I0640691

Penguin Education

Penguin Education Specials
General Editor : Willem van der Eyken

The Pre-School Years
Willem van der Eyken

Willem van der Eyken was born in Indonesia of Dutch
parents, brought up in South Africa and settled in Europe.
He has been education correspondent of the London *Evening
Standard,* founded *New Education* and was education
correspondent of the *Financial Times.* He edited a report on
Education Research and the Teacher for the National
Foundation for Educational Research, carried out research for
the UNESCO report on the effects of apartheid, and is
co-author, with Barry Turner, of *Adventures in Education*
(Allen Lane The Penguin Press, 1969). He is Senior Research
Fellow in the Further Education Group at Brunel University.

Penguin Education
Special

The Pre-School Years
Willem van der Eyken

Penguin Books   Second Edition

351660

Penguin Books Ltd, Harmondsworth,
Middlesex, England
Penguin Books Inc., 7110 Ambassador Road,
Baltimore, Md 21207, U.S.A.
Penguin Books Australia Ltd, Ringwood,
Victoria, Australia

First published 1967
Reprinted 1968
Second edition 1969
Reprinted 1971
Copyright © Willem van der Eyken, 1967, 1969

Made and printed in Great Britain by
Hazell Watson & Viney Ltd,
Aylesbury, Bucks
Set in Monotype Plantin

Contents

Preface to the Second Edition

In the two years since *The Pre-School Years* was first published, so much has happened in this field that to embrace all the developments would involve a very large volume. The changes are reflected in the new reference section: in 1967 it took up three pages, in this edition it is five times as long.

Inevitably, it is not possible to deal comprehensively with all the new advances. In this volume, the statistics for pre-schooling have been expanded, and their analysis carried out in greater detail. There is a new chapter on the geography of deprivation and another new chapter on the provision of nursery schooling now under way in Britain. The list of organizations concerned with the young child has been very largely extended and revised. There is a new chapter on the theory of play, and where possible the text reflects developments in the continuing debate on the growth of intelligence in the very young. The revised edition also includes many suggestions made by readers of the earlier version. These have been welcome.

Indeed, only one general factor has not changed. That is the provision made by the State for the education of the under-fives. One critic suggested that the book kicked 'against an open door'. Perhaps – but few are being let through.

Willem van der Eyken,
May 1969

Glossary

Adventure Playground A play area that has not been planned, but where materials such as wood, sand, bricks, old tyres and 'junk' are present for children to use imaginatively.

Bewahranstalten A German form of nursery, accepting children mainly from working mothers, and taking them into care.

Crèche Originally a French idea, a *crèche* accepts babies of working mothers for the full day, but is not geared to make any educational provision for them.

Day Nursery This is basically for older pre-school children whose mothers are away or at work. It merely seeks to look after children and does not have an education function. Often provided by industry to help female staff.

Child Minder A person who looks after children, usually in her own home and for a fee, while mothers are out to work. Has to be registered.

École Maternelle The French equivalent of the kindergarten, which enrols children as young as two years of age and takes them until they move, at six, to the *école primaire*. The *école maternelle* provides a rich educational environment.

Jardins des Enfants The Belgian equivalent of the kindergarten.

Kindergarten The creation of Friedrich Froebel, it originally was a place which embodied his mystic philosophy that childhood is not simply a preparation for adulthood, but an essential aspect of the Divine Unity. Now commonly used as a generic term for any school taking pre-school children and giving them a 'child-orientated' approach to learning.

Krippe The German equivalent of the *crèche*, often sponsored by industry.

Nursery An ambivalent term, which might be applied to any place where young children are looked after. Sometimes it applies to a room in a large house, but more usually it is an abbreviation for day nursery.

Nursery classes These are special classes attached to infant schools where children of pre-school age are introduced to an educational environment.

Nursery school The word 'school' is misleading. There are no formal lessons, but children from two to five are supervised by trained staff and given a stimulating environment in which, through self-discovery, they can broaden their outlook.

Playgroup A group normally run by parents, who charge a small fee for each child, to provide a degree of recreation and stimulus for local children.

It is a great mistake to think of the Nursery School idea
merely – or even mainly – in terms of health,
or to be satisfied with leaving its practical development
to a few enthusiasts, or to the provident Local Authorities,
or to the mitigation of life in a slum. It belongs fundamentally
to the question of whether a civilized community is possible
or not.

(*Education Enquiry Committee*, 1929)

The under-fives are the only age group for whom no extra
educational provision of any kind has been made since
1944. . . . Nursery education on a large scale remains an
unfulfilled promise.

(*Children and their Primary Schools*, 1967)

Chapter One
Two Crucial Facts

When historians come to chronicle the changes that have taken place in society in the second half of the twentieth century, one of the features that will strike them most forcibly is the wide recognition of the importance of education. This is true not only of Western industrialized countries but of the still developing nations of Africa, Asia and Latin America, where comparatively large and hard-earned sums are being allocated to schooling.

This is partly a recognition that education is a vital factor in the growth of any nation's economy. Partly it is the result of modern politics, that has created new independent nations out of former colonial territories. But perhaps most important of all it is a sign that people have come to see education as a worthwhile pursuit, something to be undertaken for its own sake.

But this new recognition is also accompanied by an extraordinarily vague view of the ultimate purpose of education, quite unlike the hard, practical approach of many earlier cultures. The Greeks wanted to produce philosophers, and directed their education towards that end. The Romans sought to train members of the senate. The early church provided education as a training for the clergy. The British education system of the nineteenth century was aimed at producing legislators and colonial administrators. Those who devised these education systems knew what they wanted, and saw to it that they produced the right results. By contrast, a country like England, which this year will spend more than £2000 million, or 6 per cent of its national income, on education, has only just begun to question whether the subjects that are taught in school are the right ones, and whether the ways in which knowledge is transmitted are the most efficient.

So although today we spend an unprecedented amount of money on education, we have lost sight of our objectives in our desire to provide for all. What most people would now claim for the system is that the simple fact of exposure to the experience of school does children good, that it enables some to pass the necessary examinations they need to further their careers and that it gives the majority a passable understanding of the world and some useful skills in dealing with the problems of adult life.

Even these limited objectives, however, are being pursued within a system largely designed for quite different purposes; a system which has been inherited rather than purpose-built, and which resorts to tradition, force of habit and folklore to achieve its results. The outcome is that we not only fail to achieve our goals in education, but that, in a crucial respect, the education system we have prevents us from achieving the very aims it is supposed to realize.

The central thesis of this book is that if we are really serious about educating our youth, if we really want to obtain positive value for our £2000 million a year, if we see the education system of a nation as more than an euphoric experience through which every child should pass, then our efforts should be concentrated on a group of some five millions who are not included in the system at all. These are the children who, at present, do not fall at all under the aegis of the Department of Education and Science, although all the evidence of science points to the fact that they, above all, would benefit most from education. They are, quite simply, very young children.

This is by no means a new thesis. It is, indeed, strikingly old. Throughout this book, therefore, the accent will not be on the novelty of the idea, but on the weight of the evidence, as it has been built up over the years.

Consider, for example, the story of Karl Witte. By any yardstick, young Karl was a prodigy of amazing potential. Born to the clergyman of a small German village in 1800, this remarkable child was giving public demonstrations of his ability to read Italian, French, German and Latin at seven, and enrolled at the University of Leipzig at the age of nine. He became a Doctor of Laws at sixteen, and a professor at Berlin University soon after.

The striking feature of his childhood was the attitude of his father. For when Karl was born, Pastor Witte decided to devote his entire life to the education of his son. 'My whole work,' he wrote later, 'is intended to prove to the intelligent person that the schoolmaster, no matter how well endowed with knowledge and the ability to teach, is, in spite of his best wishes, unable to accomplish anything if others have previously worked against him, or still continue to work against him.'

What Pastor Witte said in 1800 could, without amendment, have found a place in the Plowden Committee Report.

Very few of the child's responses are wholly innate; most require learning, though the basis on which learning can take place is inborn. The baby depends on environmental stimuli for his development, and these need to be varied and complex if the full range of normal behaviour is to be developed. It is the function of the educational process to provide these stimuli from the moment of birth onwards.

(*Children and their Primary Schools*, 1967, para. 42.)

That was Pastor Witte's belief too. From the moment Karl was born, his parents bent over him in constant attendance. They played with him. They talked to him. They named parts of his body, areas of the room, everyday objects. They took him for walks and pointed out the names of trees and plants, and discussed how these differed in height and shape. The young child was exposed to an endless array of experiences, from concerts to the theatre from the opera to the zoo. Questions were encouraged, and answers provided. Between three and four, he was taught to read and a year later he taught himself to write. All this effort – and there has seldom been a case of more dedicated parents – was noted down in a book of more than 1000 pages by the ambitious father, whose views, judging by the subsequent success of his son, triumphed. Or was this an isolated case of an eccentric man deciding to spend an inordinate time on a baby who turned out, by coincidence, to be a prodigy?

What is indisputable is that Pastor Witte understood, as many have since his day, the value of a stimulating environment for the very young child. Teachers like Froebel and

Maria Montessori have taught us the same lesson, and few today would deny that an environment that encourages the imagination of the small but fast-growing pre-school child, that supports its first stumbling movements into fresh fields of inquiry, that puts it in contact with a variety of phenomena and that stimulates its dawning control of language, thereby actively helps it to grow. We know from the studies made of identical twins – that is, children with a similar genetic inheritance – that the environment plays a very large part in the development of any child. Such twins, sharing a common home life, show a closely related level of intelligence in later life. But if they are reared apart in environments that differ widely, their levels of intelligence, although still related, are far less closely matched.

That much is common knowledge. What is less well-known, or at least less widely recognized, is that this stimulating environment does not have an even effect throughout child-hood. Intelligence is a factor that does not develop regularly over the years but shows a dramatic initial rise that gradually tails off and comes to a halt as we reach maturity. The same is true for height. We know that boys and girls grow very fast at certain periods in their lives and that, in particular, girls between eleven and twelve, and boys between thirteen and fourteen suddenly shoot upwards as their bodies respond to the chemical changes taking place within them.

Intelligence, too, has its optimum growth periods, but in this case the stages of development do not match those for height. In a study of a large group of children made over the period from their birth to their eighteenth birthday, an American sociologist tested the intelligence of these children at every step. She found that, as with height, development ceased at about seventeen years of age, but that the first four or five years were more critical for intelligence than for height.

At the age of three, for example, a child has reached roughly half the height he will attain as an adult, and by the age of twelve, approximately four-fifths. With intelligence, the rate of development is significantly different: one-fifth of the adult level is achieved in the first year of life, nearly half by the fourth birthday, and about 80 per cent by the age of eight.

Now a study like this comes under immediate criticism over the obvious difficulties of trying to measure intelligence in very young children, but in subsequent attempts to repeat the results, the main pattern of development seems to have been verified (Bloom, 1964). If these studies are correct, we are armed with two important facts: that a rich environment has a marked and measurable effect on the intellectual growth of children and that this environment is likely to be particularly crucial in the early stages of a child's life, when intelligence appears to be developing at the fastest rate.

We can, moreover, assume that the effects of the environment are irreversible: that is to say, whatever benefits or handicaps are bestowed by the environment on a young child cannot entirely be removed by subsequent experience, just as a child which has grown to four feet as a result of its own development, supplemented by good food, fresh air and sunshine, will not actually grow smaller even if it subsequently falls on hard times.

These are crucial facts, for on the use we make of them depends the quality of people our education system sets out, at such enormous cost, to develop. We are no longer talking about the possibility of making certain provisions for young children but instead are debating the kind of society we desire, the kind of priorities within that society which will be advanced, the kind of life we wish to be pursued. They are issues which move out of the realm of education and concern the very fabric of our civilization. In that sense, they are universal and timeless.

But the facts also have a particular relevance to events today, for while our education system (and society in general) pays lip-service to the sentiments of Pastor Witte that a child's early environment is critical to its later development, the environment itself is changing at a rapid rate. In doing so, it is becoming an environment that is inimical to the young child, foreign to its needs, oblivious of its demands. It is necessary, therefore, to look at the kind of society that is being shaped by modern technology and to contrast this with what we now know about the essential requirements for the full intellectual growth of young children. That contrast, I believe, is stark.

Chapter Two
The Changing Environment

Throughout Europe societies are at work changing their education systems. What they are doing, basically, is to reform élitist systems, designed to educate small groups of privileged children from specially favoured families, into systems that are democratic in character and in which, ideally, every child, whatever its innate ability, its home background or its inclinations, can achieve its maximum potential. Slowly, in the face of understandable conservative traditions and the fact that elaborate administrative structures already exist, they are striving to implement the memorable phrase contained in the Hadow report: 'What a good and wise parent will desire for his own children, a nation must desire for all children.'

Behind these changes lies the more fundamental political belief in an equality of opportunity for all. Throughout the whole history of revolutionary politics, from Vico to the present day, there lies a search for a form of government that could provide such equality. In the words of the historian Saint-Simon: 'All my life may be summed up in one idea: to guarantee to all men the free development of their faculties.' Mr Anthony Crosland, in his book *The Future of Socialism* (p. 140), has put it another way:

Most liberal people would now allow that every child has a natural 'right' as citizen, not merely to 'life, liberty and the pursuit of happiness' but to that position in the social scale to which his native talents entitle him; should have, in other words, an equal opportunity for wealth, advancement and renown. Complete achievement of this is, of course, an unattainable ideal; for the children of talented parents start with a pronounced environmental advantage. But subject only to this, all children can, if the society so decided, at least be given an equal chance of access to the best education.

The older the education system, the more painful are the

transformations associated with a move towards this philosophy. In England and Wales, with an educational tradition that stretches unbroken from the great church schools of Canterbury and York of the eleventh century, it is bound to be traumatic. New universities to challenge the ancient rights of the old; new forms of schools to replace the older grammar tradition. Even the length of schooling is being altered.

But it is not just the education system that is changing; society itself is evolving. One of the factors making for change is simply that our island is getting more crowded. One hundred years ago, there were 24,500,000 people in the United Kingdom. Fifty years ago the number had risen to 43,000,000. Today, there are 56,000,000. That means more people occupying proportionally less land, and attracted increasingly away from the rural areas to the big cities, so that the burden of absorbing these extra numbers has fallen heavily and directly on the major conurbations.

Such pressure has had a visible effect on the environment. The West Midlands area, for example, built 13,000 dwellings in 1956. Ten years later, it had to put up 17,500 and still could not cope with the demand. In the Greater London area, 50 per cent more buildings were put up in 1966 than ten years previously. In many cases, of course, these new homes simply took the place of older buildings that were pulled down. But the land cleared in this way has by no means provided enough space to meet the demand, and the constant clamour has been for more space on which to build yet more houses.

The only answer to this incessant appetite has been to build upwards. Everywhere, the skyline of England is being changed as massed blocks of flats, linked by roadways, shopping precincts, car parks and all the paraphernalia of modern life, rise up. It has been a frenetic development. In 1953, the highest flat building in Britain rose a modest fourteen storeys into the sky. By 1966, more than 6600 blocks with more than twenty storeys each were put up in that year alone, introducing an entirely new way of life for many people who had been brought up in a single or double-storied house, with a small yard at the back and perhaps a patch of garden in the front.

The enquiry into the collapse of one of these tall buildings at Ronan Point in the London borough of Newham in May, 1968 revealed that until the mid-1950s, the London boroughs built mainly two-storey houses and three-storey flats at relatively low densities of about 70 people per acre.

But there was then a radical change of policy and schemes were designed at densities of up to 140–50 persons per acre. This resulted in about 75 per cent of dwellings being provided in high blocks of flats ranging from eight to twenty-three storeys and 25 per cent in three- or four-bedroom houses, suitable for large families. (Para. 20, *Report of the Enquiry into the Collapse of Flats at Ronan Point, Canning Town*, H.M.S.O., 1968.)

This kind and speed of development has created a major change in our social environment, and done so almost overnight. Between 1945 and 1960 only about one-fifth of all the dwellings built in England and Wales were flats. In 1965, more than half of all the houses put up in that year were flats. And the transformation has hardly begun. It has been estimated that by 1972, dwellings in high blocks in the Greater London area alone will reach the figure of 18,000, housing a population of more than 50,000. That may not seem a very large figure when placed against the total number of people living in the area, but it represents a dramatic increase and points the way the environment will develop. Of this estimated population more than 3000 will be children between the ages of one and five years.

A sociologist, writing in the *Housing Centre Review*, pointed out:

One aspect of designing flats which has not hitherto been given sufficient attention is that of providing adequately and imaginatively for children's play. Very many comments have been made as to the undesirability of bringing up children in flats and general regrets are expressed that this should occur at all; nevertheless, with the present density standards for inner and middle rings of London, large numbers of children will inevitably be spending their most formative years on flatted estates. It is therefore of urgent importance that a suitable environment should be planned for them. (Willis, 1953.)

'I never let him go out by himself,' said one mother, when asked about the way she managed to cope with her child in a tall flat building. 'The balcony worries me to death – I don't let them out of my sight.'

'It's very awkward – there's nowhere for them to play,' said another young mother to an investigator (Maizels, 1961). 'We can't let them out. It is a pressing problem in the winter. We get no let-up from the children, and for those under school age, it's terrible. The children feel hemmed in.'

In the brave new world of the towering housing estates, the lives of young children, far from being liberated, are circumscribed. The new environment being created by the planners may be suitable for fast traffic, for adults and for architects; it is antagonistic to the whole development of young children. Here is a random sample of how they spend their young days.

A girl of three, living on the twelfth floor of a block of flats:

Had breakfast – played in flat – sister-in-law and her boy of four came on visit – played for about three hours with their toys – stayed to dinner – then went shopping – had extra walk to kill time – came home – had tea – friend called with boy of two – watched T.V. and then bed.

A boy of four, living on the tenth floor:

Played with his toys in his room – went to shops for about half an hour – then he played by himself – after dinner played by himself – then we went to the recreation ground for about one hour – came back and watched T.V. for about half an hour with a friend from next door – went to bed about six-thirty.

A girl of three, living on the seventh floor:

Got up – played indoors – went shopping for about half an hour – did the washing downstairs with mother – came and had her dinner. Then had a sleep for one and a half hours – watched T.V. – had tea – got ready for bed.

A survey, carried out a few years ago at the London School of Economics on families living high in new blocks of flats, showed that most of these people were pleased with many of the features of their new homes. They provided considerable views, offered more privacy, reduced the level of noise and were thought to be, on the whole, 'healthier' (Maizels, 1961).

'But a majority also thought it was less easy to enjoy surrounding open spaces and gardens, and two-fifths of those approached complained of loneliness.' The survey, conducted by Professor Peter Townsend, showed that the chief preoccupation of the mothers was with safety, and the lack of socializing and educational opportunities for their young children. Only twenty-five out of eighty-eight people said that a playground was available near their particular flat building, and of these, twenty-two admitted that there was no adult supervision at the ground. Four-fifths of the others said that a playground with supervision was needed. Overwhelming demand existed among these parents for some kind of playroom within the building, and three-quarters of them said they wanted a nursery school.

Describing the life in one of these tower blocks in an article in the *Guardian*, 10 October 1966, Tony Geraghty commented:

Mothers suffer, too. The isolation of living above 100 feet with children whose hunger for play space and company makes some of them long wistfully for the happier times in the creaking place from which they were moved. . . . There is a play space; a tiny 'adventure' playground, which consists of concentric rings of concrete wall, or concrete stepping stones. Mothers, tired of the wails of their offspring who fall and batter their faces on these devices, are wary of the playground. Older children prefer the street a few feet away. . . .

The modern environments that we are creating in this way are not the friends of children; indeed, the architects who are creating them have scarcely thought about the needs of the young who will live their first, impressionable years in these hollow towers, deprived of the chance of raising pets, or rushing outside at the first fall of snow, of dancing around a bonfire or making the first, tentative attempts to ride a bicycle. Most of all, they deprive a child of what is probably the most important single influence in his young years – the informal and casual contact not only with other children of their own age, but with adults and older children, all of them potential enemies, with whom the child must form working relationships that provide him with both protection and a springboard for the making of deeper friendships. In the end the indictment of these environments is simply that they are anti-child; that they demand of the young a type of behaviour – acquiescent, silent, estranged – that is the very antithesis of the inherent nature of childhood.

But if the environment of tomorrow is anti-child, there is not much to be said either for the environment of today. For millions of children growing up in Britain in 1967 life is still a matter of relative poverty. Professor Peter Townsend (1967) has reported that between seven and eight million persons, or about 14 per cent of the total population, live below a specifically defined 'national assistance' standard. As these lower-income groups often have the largest families, it could be that something like one-fifth of the child population of Britain grows up in an environment that in certain fundamental respects can be classed as 'deprived'.

Moreover, even if the home itself is not in this category, the area in which the child lives may well be. The Plowden Committee Report drew specific attention to what it called 'educational priority areas' (*Children and their Primary Schools,* 1967, para. 131).

Some of these neighbourhoods have for generations been starved of new schools, new houses and new investment of every kind. Everyone knows this; but for year after year priority has been given to the new towns and new suburbs, because if new schools do not keep pace with the new houses some children will be unable to go to school at all. (*Children and their Primary Schools,* 1967, para. 132.)

A primary school head teacher, talking about children in such areas (*Trends in Education,* 1966), said this:

'Do you know, we even have to teach some of these children how to play. When they first come here they sit around with vacant expressions. Communication by them and with them is non-existent. In the infants, we get some children that aren't even toilet-trained – at five! In twilight areas, nursery schools are almost essential. Contact between the children and people other than their parents cannot start young enough.'

The head teacher went on to explain some of the problems of running a school in such an area.

'The kind of teaching we need is different with these children, too, as their mothers have never told them bedtime stories. They need to be told stories very frequently. In this way they become more interested in books and ask to see the pictures. Then they want to talk about the pictures and plenty of time should be allowed for this. Many, coming from homes where parents have no time to talk to them or take any interest in answering their questions, find normal conversation strange. Their most crying need is communication, so situations must be created where they can talk and ask questions.

They need plenty of space so that they can run about and skip and enjoy themselves. They need to be able to shout and sing, which often they can't do at home, as father is in bed as he is on night shift. They need to hear good music at their own level. They need to be able to have the joy of moving to music, and so each school should have at least one good pianist as well as a gramophone, wireless and tape recorder. They need to be able to dress up as all generations of children before them have done. This should lead naturally on to free drama among themselves, and not for an audience.

Deprivation can take many guises. It can mean living in over-crowded conditions, being deafened by the noise of aeroplanes or constantly passing trains, living in smoke-enshrouded communities or being brought up in a society to which the world of books, sophisticated conversation, peace and contemplation or the challenge of intellectual problems is foreign.

The degree to which at least some of these elements are present throughout our society is frightening. J. W. B. Douglas and J. M. Blomfield (1958), two members of a joint committee sponsored by the Institute of Child Health, the

Society of Medical Officers of Health and the Population Investigation Committee, found, in following up a representative sample of 5000 babies born in 1946, that only 7 per cent had parents who had both enjoyed the benefits of secondary education. In this respect, at least, our society has made headway. But they also found that 26 per cent of the four-year-old children in England and Wales were sharing their beds either with brothers or sisters, or, in some cases, with an adult. Only 29 per cent of them had a room of their own. Nor was this always a direct result of overcrowding. Even among the professional and salaried non-manual workers, where financial circumstances were better, or in families where there was no evident deprivation, bed-sharing was still often a necessity.

One particularly revealing point from this survey was the degree to which mothers were efficient in caring for their children. Douglas and Blomfield and their co-workers considered how health visitors rated the mother's management of her child, the adequacy of the child's shoes, clothes, the cleanliness of the child and of its home. Using a composite code for these different factors (best, intermediate and worst) it was found that even among the professional and salaried non-manual workers, only two-thirds of the mothers fell into the 'best' group. There was a marked decline of standards in the lower-income groups, and over all nearly half the total (some 43 per cent) were rated 'worst', Child welfare centres were never used by 28 per cent of the families, and another 59 per cent used them only irregularly.

Although the statistics of the 1958 survey are to some extent out of date, I have quoted them to show that the elements of a bad environment are by no means confined to the families of the poor, or the ill-educated, or the badly housed. There is, in addition, another factor which as a result of increasing affluence works against the welfare of the young child: the growing army of mothers who are now going out to work.

Professor Peter Townsend has said (1967, p. 12) that 'the number of wives in paid employment has been rising steadily since the war and is now around four and a half millions'. The Douglas and Blomfield survey (1958, p. 117) showed that the proportion of mothers in regular employment (that is to say, at least thirty-five hours a week) during the pre-school period of their children was about 26 per cent. Since that survey was carried out, the 1961 General Census has revealed, for the first time, the true extent of this labour force. It showed that, of the 2,500,000 women in the country with children under five, 314,000 had jobs of one kind or another and that, of these, 140,000 were actually in full-time employment (*Household Composition Tables*, 1966, Table 41). But even of those in part-time employment, the majority (103,000) worked between twelve and thirty hours a week. In other words, 5 per cent of all mothers with pre-school children go out to full-time employment, and another 6 per cent have part-time work, the majority of them for fairly long periods. When one asks what happens to the children themselves, as Douglas did, one finds that while about 17 per cent are in day nurseries or nursery classes, the vast majority are left in the care of relatives, friends or paid helps (Douglas and Blomfield, 1958).

To the eternal optimist it might seem reasonable to argue that when we have taken away the special problems connected with working mothers, excluded the equally special cases of children living in high flats, eliminated the poverty factor, and made allowances for children living in distressed areas – when a blind eye is turned to all these aspects – there still remains a vast bulk of the population which is presumably providing a reasonable environment for its young children. That is to misread the evidence. The point I was to make here is that, however enlightened, financially secure and socially aware the parents, however affluent the neighbourhood, the home environment provided for the pre-school child is inadequate if measured in absolute terms against the child's potential social and intellectual development during this period, and that it takes the dedication of a Pastor Witte, coupled with the social mixing which even he failed to provide, to do justice to the demands of the under-fives.

Yet what we observe of social change today seems to be moving positively in the opposite direction. Among the top strata of society adults appear to have less time available for their children, and at the lower end economic pressures force the mother to take a job and neglect her children. In the vast middle of our society there is a kind of silence, a lack of communication and a sense of isolation that the pre-war tenement blocks, for all their hazards to health, never knew. Not homes, but hutches, each a neat, tidy island in a straggling archipelago of suburbia; identical and faceless.

It is easy to make dogmatic statements of this kind, but difficult to provide any kind of quantitive analysis to back them up. One indication of the kind of isolation I mean can be seen in the letters which – at the rate of twenty a day – pour into the offices of a television programme like 'Play School', produced by the B.B.C. particularly for the under-fives.

Although this programme runs for only twenty-five minutes the impact it has made goes far beyond its relatively small viewing public. A harassed mother writes:

I am knee-deep in washing, the baby is bawling to be fed and the hands of the kitchen clock rush relentlessly towards lunch time. My $2\frac{1}{2}$-year-old boy is furious if he ever has to miss the programme. I enjoy twenty-five minutes' peace while it is on – but that is the least of my reasons for writing. Educationally, I think the programme is splendid. It provides me with numerous ideas for extending play throughout the day. . . .

Here, in what sociologists would describe as a 'good home environment', we catch a glimpse not merely of the difficulty of coping both with housework and children, but of the need for supplementing the cultural equipment of parents.

A poignant picture of isolation was contained in this letter:

I am a nurse looking after a highly intelligent, though lonely little girl of three whose parents are both university lecturers. After her third birthday in May we started watching 'Play School', and I can honestly say it is the highlight of our day. We watched the repeat of the second birthday celebration today and my rather sober little charge rocked with laughter at the antics of the cow'.

Sometimes the programme, just by presenting material in an interesting way, achieves more than the efforts of even a concerned mother.

When I try to teach David anything he is like a resentful block of wood, but since he has watched your programme I realize as I hear him talking in his games that he has a good memorie (*sic*) and takes in most of what you tell him. I feel sure that by the time he starts school in January next year he will have learned quite a lot. . . .

Quite inadvertently, parents writing to the producers of such a programme reveal insights into the daily lives of their young children.

I only wish that there were more programmes like this during the day, as I find at this age, children can get rather bored with just playing. . . .

Our little boy, although only two last July, often joins in the songs and action games and his knowledge of nursery rhymes and songs has been much extended by your programme.

My own four-year-old daughter and all her friends are enthralled with the series – by four years the children have grown bored and become over-familiar with 'Andy Pandy', the 'Woodentops', etc., and welcome the stimulus of something such as 'Play School'.

It is noticeable, reading letters such as this, how even the vicarious stimulus provided by a short but excellent programme of this kind actively enhances the cultural and intellectual appetite of children. Here is a comment that reflects the views of many parents:

I feel I must write and tell you how much my son, who is aged three and a half, enjoys 'Play School'. Until about six months ago he was quite content with 'Watch with Mother' but now needs something more stimulating.

Another way to measure the effect that our social environment has on young children is to conduct a survey among reception classes at infant schools to judge, for example, the level of maturity and social integration among the children arriving at the school for the first time. It was not possible to conduct a survey for this book, but I did take the opportunity of speaking to about twenty reception class teachers in various parts of the country to seek their views. These differed widely, depending on the particular area involved, but what was notable was their general accord about certain fundamental points.

They all said that five-year-olds who come to school today have none of the rich subculture of fairy stories, games, rhymes and tales that children used to possess. Instead, they were armed with a veneer of television culture and advertising copy that had no depth, humour or applicability to their own situation. ('Remember,' the American educator Dr Lloyd J. Trump once told an audience, 'that children come to our schools with an exposure of 3000 hours of television.')

More important, perhaps, is that they do not enjoy conversation in their homes. One small boy in a reception class, asked if his mother had heard him read a passage of his book at home, replied: 'Yes, but she was watching television at the time.'

The result is that many infant teachers find that the children who come to school for the first time at the age of five, or approaching their fifth birthday, often have great difficulty in verbally communicating either with other children or with the staff. This leads to frustration, feelings of inferiority, and in turn provides a handicap in learning to read.

The third factor about which reception class teachers seem to be unanimous is the limited range of experience enjoyed by the children who come to them. One teacher in a school situated within ten miles of London was case-hardened to the fact that most of her pupils had never been to Trafalgar Square or the Tower of London, but was amazed to learn that more than half of them had not been to the largest local park, either. Another teacher told me that when she took her children on an outing it was revealed that for more than half of her class this was the first time they had ever travelled on a train.

All these shortcomings might be ignored as imperfections in a world which can never hope to provide perfect conditions for any individual, no matter how great our concern or how deep our purse; it might be, that is, if it were not for the two facts which we now possess about the intellectual development and social growth of young children.

So long as intellectual differences were seen mainly as the result of genetic variations about which society could do nothing, or of elements of chance, or of individual characteristics that were not the responsibility of society, it was justifiable to ignore the early years of a child's life beyond the rudimentary controls of sanitation and basic hygiene, and concentrate attention on improving the educational facilities for its later years. But 'as the causal relations between the environment and individual development become more clearly defined, it will be difficult for individuals or social institutions to idly observe events taking their course,' remarks Professor Benjamin Bloom (1964, p. 227), Professor of Education at the University of Chicago and one of the first two elected members of the U.S. National Academy of Education whose book, *Stability and Change in Human Characteristics*, is probably the most important single work to be written on the subject.

We live in a society which depends, as we are daily reminded, upon the native skills of its people. Moreover, we live in a society that creates its own environment. It is we who ask children to grow in a world that is laden with smog, that is full of unwanted, terrifying sound and clatter, that is overcrowded and busy. This is not the work of nature, or of some external machinations over which we have no control. We could change it if we wanted to. But we are too preoccupied.

Recognizing this, we have embarked on a large expenditure of money and of people to make education as comprehensive as possible. We are changing our system to a more egalitarian, more open one in the pious belief that this is the way to provide justice and an equality of opportunity for all. But there is no egalitarianism in a system which provides riches at sixteen when, at four or five, a child has been too impoverished to take advantage of them.

On the basis of a great deal of research, some of which will be described here, it is now possible to predict, with increasing accuracy, the shape, size and to some extent the intellectual growth and emotional development of future adults from their characteristics as children. For example, most children attain 54 per cent of their adult height in the first three years of their lives, so that it is fairly simple to predict at a very early age how tall they will grow. We can even predict how much a balanced diet and a healthy environment will affect this growth, so that the estimate can be remarkably accurate. Using similar techniques it is now thought possible to predict for very young children of six years or less how they will fit into our society, whether they will be intelligent or dull, anti-social or responsible. This is a weapon that carries with it a new responsibility.

As Professor Bloom puts it (1964, p. 231):

If school drop-outs, delinquent behavior and frustration with the educational requirements of a society can be predicted long in advance, can we sit idly by and watch the prophesies come true? If remedial actions and therapy are less effective at later stages in the individual's development, can we satisfy a social conscience by indulging in such activities when it is far too late?

Put briefly, the increased ability to predict long-term consequences of environmental forces and developmental chacteristics places new responsibilities on the home, the school and the society. If these responsibilities are not adequately met, society will suffer in the long run. If these responsibilities are neglected, the individual will suffer a life of continual frustration and alienation.

These are strong words, placing a very large responsibility upon society. The question is: are they justified? Those in sympathy with the general thesis often assume that the early years are important, without considering closely just what it is that is important about them. Those fundamentally opposed to the uncomfortable idea that our education systems are wholly irrational make a second assumption which dismisses this period as one consisting largely of maturational events which have little or nothing to do with education. To anyone concerned to convince both sides, the weapons at hand are few. We probably know more about the face of the moon than about the development of children. But our ignorance is far from total, and if we are to understand the extent of the problem we must first of all make an attempt to see whether we can unravel some of the main traits of child development.

A human being is the most complicated piece of biological engineering in the world, and its development, from the first fertilization of the female egg through to the incredibly long growth period of some eighteen years to the full-grown adult, is one that baffles the imagination.

The complexity of the human brain, in particular, is one to inspire awe. It has been described as equivalent to a computer with 10^9 elements contained in a package occupying about one-tenth of a cubic foot, weighing only three and a half pounds. But the now common practice of comparing the human brain to a computer is a scandalous exercise in over-simplification. For the brain's elements provide a private biological factory that not only gives off continuous power but which feeds in a constant and diverse array of information for sorting, analysis and action. Moreover, the brain, unlike any computer, has the whole history of its development wrapped up in itself. It is as if the Concorde airliner had built into its own structure not only the airframes of earlier airliners, but the wooden struts used by the Wright brothers as well.

Not only does the brain contain a vast number of elements or brain cells, many of which have very special functions, but each of these cells can, in theory, communicate with its neighbour to form a pathway and so create a network whose range defies calculation. It has been worked out that if the elements were limited to a million the number of different two-cell links that could be formed would amount to $10^{2,783,000}$, a number so vast that it would fill several books of this size just to write down. But the actual number of nerve cells is nearer 10,000 million!

In a famous quotation, Sir Charles Sherrington, one of the great research workers on the brain, once described it as 'an enchanted loom, where millions of flashing shuttles weave a dissolving pattern, always a meaningful pattern, though never an abiding one.' Only eight weeks after conception, the rudiments of this loom are at work, and by the seventh foetal month, it is possible to record some electrical activity from the growing brain. Because the evidence from these electrical impulses may in time lead to a greater understanding of the development of what we call intelligence and the phenomenon of learning, it is worthwhile considering them in greater detail.

The idea that the brain generates electrical impulses came in 1875 to a thirty-three-year-old Liverpool doctor, Richard Caton, who showed in experiments on dogs and rabbits that when electrodes were placed in their brains, not only were weak electric current recorded on a galvanometer, but these current varied when the animals were exposed to different stimuli. Since that time a great deal of work has been done in recording these currents using a machine called an electro-encephalograph (EEG). Because these recordings are the nearest we can get to a living photograph of the growing brain, their study, particularly in the early years of a child's life, could be very revealing.

The Plowden Committee Report (*Children and their Primary Schools*, 1967) mentions in its opening chapter the concept of certain critical periods in a child's life when, for no clear reason, learning is at its height. The theory is that, at certain times during the development of any living organism, such periods exist during which responses to the environment are potentially very dramatic and which, if not made at that stage, might be missed for ever. One fascinating example of such a critical period is 'imprinting', the phenomenon in which animals follow the first large and friendly object they see soon after birth. Normally speaking this object is the mother, and because this relationship is vital to the survival of the young and cannot wait upon a more elaborate, slow-developing relationship, it appears as if a trigger is set off within the young bird or mammal to ensure that this relationship will take place. Sometimes, however, this has disastrous results, for even if the object is not the mother, but a marauding animal or a human being, the young still makes the same attachment, and will follow the object as if it were its own mother (Sluckin, 1965).

The Plowden Committee Report mentioned another

example to show that these critical periods not only occur at highly specific times, but that their results are irreversible. They quoted the case of the first few days of the life of a rat, during which the testes of the male secrete a substance which passes to the brain and in some ways alters the structure of the hypothalamus. Once this change has occurred, the animal grows up as a male, but if the process is retarded for even a few days, regardless of the amount of substance afterwards introduced into the hypothalamus, the sex of the rat remains indeterminate. There exists a critical period, beyond which aid or reinforcement is meaningless. A similar example is given by Illingworth (1966) of red squirrels who, if not given nuts to crack at a certain age, never acquire the skill of cracking them later.

Now if animals have these hypersensitive periods when they acquire skills which are essential to their survival, it is almost certain that young children do as well. Maria Montessori, for example, insisted that in her experiments with children she found a greater receptivity in learning involving the sensory system, such as the learning of colour, shape, sound and texture, between the ages of two and a half and six than at any other time.

If we refer back to the records made of the electrical impulses of the brain, it is possible to see any of these cricital periods in action, and if so, can we then discover just when they occur? In 1955, an American team headed by Robert J. Ellingson at the Nebraska Psychiatric Institute, Omaha, began to record the electrical brain patterns of 1146 newborn babies in the hospital. For the following seven years the developing children were measured repeatedly in the same way, and later regular measurements were maintained until they were teenagers. What Ellingson and his workers saw from these tracings was that one of the wave rhythms – the alpha rhythm – suddenly increased in intensity towards the first year of a child's life. This alpha rhythm first makes its appearance in the third or fourth month of a baby's development, but at that stage has a frequency of only three or four waves per second; very feeble. Then suddenly towards the end of the first year, it leaps up to five or six waves per second. By ten years of age, the wave frequency has reached its maximum potential (Ellingson, 1964).

So it appears that around the twelfth month of a young child's life either something happens to spark off this enormous increase, or it takes place quite spontaneously. But whatever the cause, a sudden leap forward is made which is seemingly crucial to the whole later growth of the child. (The alpha waves are concerned, among other things, with perception.) Unfortunately, those who carry out research in child development and those who study neurology and the development of the biological processes seldom consider each other's work, but undoubtedly a time will come when these two fields of research will provide a map of such critical periods in the early life of the child.

What EEG records also show quite clearly, however, is the quite uneven development of the nervous system. To parents, there appears something deliberate and continuous in the growth of their child. They see it, at six weeks, kicking about, and then at about sixteen weeks, lifting its chest off a flat surface. By twenty weeks it can carry its weight on its forearms and by thirty-six weeks it may be moving backwards in an effort to crawl. At fifteen months it kneels without support and by two and a half years it can jump. Because these developments come in a logical sequence and over a fairly long spell, it is easy to be misled about the extraordinary changes that are taking place within the developing human during this time. A newborn baby is not a perfect miniature of an adult; it arrives in the world with some organs at a high stage of development, while others are virtually in embryo. Keyed by its genetic endowment, it has a highly developed sucking mechanism which has to be ready at birth for instant use, just as a foal is born with highly developed legs so that, on birth, it can rise at once and run at a pace that will keep it within the herd. But in other respects – those concerned, for example, with visual images – it is embryonic. As new powers are needed, so they develop. What is not needed atrophies. It is this kind of phased development which has ensured the survival of the species and which, perhaps less pronounced in others, may well have caused their death.

This unwinding of the genetic blueprint into a developed adult is inborn and beyond the influence of environment. Arnold Gesell, one of the great figures in the study of child development, studied twin girls from one year to eighteen months and gave one of them daily training in climbing and cube manipulation from the sixth to the forty-sixth week, while the other child was untrained. But all this practice and exercise did nothing to hasten the appearance of climbing and tower building, and at the end of the experiment there was no notable difference in these abilities between the two. Another research worker took sets of identical twins, one member of each being put on a potty hourly for seven hours each day after the first month of birth. The others were not allowed to sit on a potty until they were more than a year old. The achievements in control were about the same.

No amount of practice can make a child sit, walk, talk or acquire other skills until his nervous system is ready for it. On the other hand, delay in the acquisition of skills may be caused by depriving the child of opportunity to practise them when sufficient maturation has occurred. (Illingworth, 1966, p. 77.)

This kind of natural ripening, which depends on the development of the cerebral cortex, inevitably defines not only the child's physical development but also the stages of its mental growth. It is in this area that the work of the Swiss psychologist Jean Piaget has been so fundamental. What Piaget has demonstrated clearly is that whereas children of four or five are not equipped to deal with abstract mathematical concepts, these same concepts provide no difficulty some two years later, when certain other mental developments have taken place.

Through tests on his own three children, Piaget showed how the very young build up systems of their universe through experiments and experiences of pushing, pulling, sucking, moving limbs and generally exploring their environment. By eighteen months, the young baby appears to have a model of his limited world that is a coherent unit, and that provides him with a working hypothesis for his actions. This mental model has been built up over a large number of individual experiences, within the limits of his own home. Indeed, an excess of experiences at this early point in his life might well inhibit the growing child from forming such a model and leave him confused, distressed and anxious.

In the next three or four years this particular view of the world changes, expands, becomes vocalized. (A child learns his entire mother tongue in a matter of two or three years, and sometimes, if the environment is right, learns two or even three languages at once.) By seven or eight the basic structure of the child's model of the world is properly laid and he begins to make abstractions out of his widening experiences, although total abstract reasoning may not be possible until eleven or even fourteen years of age.

One of Piaget's most famous experiments to show this kind of governed mental development involved two vessels of the same shape and size, containing an equal amount of coloured liquid. When children of four or five were asked whether these two vessels held the same amount of liquid, they agreed that they did. But when the contents of one of these containers was poured into another vessel of a different size, the children, who now saw that the levels of the two liquids were no longer even, assumed that the quantities had somehow changed and that the one held either less or more than the other. They could not grasp the idea of constancy, for to them, when the form changed, the amount changed as well. Between five-and-a-half years and six, they vacillated in their answers to these questions but at seven or eight, the considered the whole question trivial and obvious, and immediately gave the right answers. For the young child of limited experience, the whole concept of number is bound up with size or volume, with something that he can touch or gauge. If a dozen flowers are carefully spaced out on a table and a coin is placed in front of every flower, the young child will acknowledge that there are as many coins as there are flowers. He can see the one-to-one relationship. But if the flowers are now bunched together and the coins spread out, this kind of visual relationship is lost to him, and the same child will insist that there are now more coins than flowers. Similarly, if two rods of the same length are placed on a table so that their ends are in line, the young child will agree that they are equally long. But if one of the rods is pushed slightly out of alignment, then the child will maintain that one of the rods is now longer than the other one. Conversely, if two lengths do begin and end at the same place, even if the one length is a straight rod and the other is a wavy piece of plasticine, the young child will insist that they are the same length, and will continue to do so even when the wavy length has been straightened out and shown to be longer than the straight rod.

Does this mean that in the pre-school years intellectual development is entirely governed by the maturation processes, and that regardless of the environment we provide, the child will not benefit from it? Few people would take this view, for it is clear that, while one does not waste time trying to teach a three-year-old quantum mechanics or modern mathematics, the intellectual stimulus and environment provided for the young child is influential and beneficial to this natural maturation process.

Development itself, if allowed to take place without the reinforcement of experience and constant use, is not enough to bring an organ into full use: what is apparently not needed atrophies. In an experiment conducted by two scientists in America (Hubel and Wiesel, 1963, p. 996) it was found, for example, that when the eyes of young kittens were lightly stitched shut at birth, left for two or three months and only then opened, the eyes did not function properly despite having reached full development some weeks earlier. What the eyes needed to become fully operational was experience and constant use.

Some research workers now believe that the whole process of thinking is itself something that has to be learned over and above the natural development of the physical equipment. 'All out studies indicate that the ability to solve problems without fumbling is not inborn but is acquired gradually,' wrote H. F. Harlow and Margaret Kuenne from their laboratory at the University of Wisconsin.

Thinking does not develop spontaneously as an expression of innate abilities; it is the end result of a long learning process. . . .

The brain is essential to thought, but the untutored brain is not enough, no matter how good a brain it may be. An untrained brain is sufficient for trial-and-error, fumble-through behavior, but only training enables an individual to think in terms of ideas and concepts. (Harlow and Kuenne, 1949.)

What led these two workers to this view was a series of experiments they carried out, mainly with monkeys, but also with pre-school children. The monkeys were given a small board on which lay two covers different in colour, size and shape. Under one of these lids lay some nuts. The object for the monkeys was to choose the right cover to pick up in order to get at the nuts first time. From this simple, basic task much more complicated problems were evolved. At first the monkeys learned purely by trial and error, without apparently seeing any connexion between the particular shape and colour and size of the object and the clue this gave to what was underneath. But as they went through problem after problem, they discovered the general concept that governed all the experiments and were able, faced with an entirely new challenge, to solve it immediately. Nursery school children from two to five were offered similar puzzles and began in much the same ways as the monkeys had done. As a group, they learned the principle of the experiments more quickly than the monkeys, but the way they learned was much the same.

We have called this process of progressive learning the formation of a 'learning set'. The subject learns an organized set of habits that enables him to meet effectively each new problem of this particular type. A single set would provide only limited aid in enabling an animal to adapt to an ever-changing environment. But a host of different sets may supply the raw material for human thinking. (Harlow and Kuenne, 1949.)

What we see here is the close relationship that exists between natural, physical development, enabling a child to cope with ideas, coupled with a spirit of enquiry, which forces him into new and richer forms of experience which in turn lead him on to higher levels of learning. This is primarily the lesson that Jean Piaget's work teaches. As Nathan Isaacs (1961) has stressed: 'The answer is simply that what Piaget is setting out to study is not the differences which different environments might make, but the *common* stages and laws of *all* children's mental growth.' The picture that Piaget paints of mental development fits no single child, but it is the backdrop to the development of all children. One can admit that all plants follow certain genetically defined paths of growth and yet agree that fertilizers add considerably to their final stature and quality. The concept of maturation, therefore, is in no way in competition with the demand for a proper environment of learning; it is complementary to it. Hence the old idea of an almost fixed age for reading readiness, for example, is as incomplete and misleading as the opposing theory put forward by one American psychologist, that children can be taught to read at virtually any age. Both statements display a profound ignorance of the true nature of intellectual development.

What I hope to have shown is that, before the child can develop mentally, certain physical features must be present, and that these unfold in a very uneven and sometimes dramatic way. When these particular phenomena occur equally dramatic opportunities for learning take place, and, if these are reinforced by the environment, apparently sudden leaps in understanding are made possible and the child's view of the world is enlarged and altogether altered, leading to yet further developments and possibilities. These are irreversible processes, but if they are not reinforced, or if the environment does not encourage their development, they atrophy or remain sluggish. The unfolding of the biological processes often creates such critical periods, during which spectacular development is possible, and beyond which it appears remedial action is only partly effective. Yet as the Plowden Committee Report has emphasized:

A critical period is only the extreme example of a more general class of sensitive periods. It is likely that, in the sphere of learning, periods of maximum sensitivity rather than of critical now-or-neverness exist. (*Children and their Primary Schools*, para. 28.)

But to talk of mental development as if it is an isolated

phenomenon is to tell only part of an inexplicably intertwined process. Learning and its application are not merely matters of opportunities grasped or of facilities provided. They are bound up with the whole psychology of the child, with his relations with his family, with his dawning realization that beyond his own world lies a far more complex one peopled by strangers, with his ability to work and play with others, with the formation of habits that bring order out of the chaos of unrelated experiences, with his ability to turn the innate anti-social behaviour of the baby into the organized social behaviour of the school child.

One of the key factors in this multiple process is the acquisition of language. It is here, in a critical sphere, that the most fruitful amalgam between environment, natural ability and physical development can be seen to take place. Because speech is a factor in a child's internal equipment for thinking, for controlling and sorting experiences and for guiding his own responses to them, its full development is fundamental to future growth.

Between two and five, a child's active vocabulary grows at a dramatic rate, reaching an average of more than 2000 words. Because it is considered that a child needs about 3000 words in his vocabulary before he is ready to start learning to read, it is imperative that the environment should be verbally rich enough to provide such development. Obviously two factors are important here; first, that the child is talked to as often as possible and stimulated to respond liguistically, and second, that the quality of conversation is such that a child is constantly expanding not merely his vocabulary but his entire range of language; that is to say, that he is weaned away from both baby-talk (if that has ever been used at all) and the simple, unambiguous forms of speech towards more sophisticated, subtle ways of using language that can convey meanings and information not available in any other way.

It has been suggested by Professor Basil Bernstein (1961) that there are, in fact, two quite distinct forms of language, and that many children, because they do not come into close contact with children outside their own social class, or because they are not spoken to enough, are limited in their early years to only one of these forms, to the future detriment of their intellectual development.

Middle-class children, believes Dr Bernstein, are brought up in an environment where language is often quite formal and where thoughts are expressed in such a way that the person expressing them is not necessarily identified with the thoughts.

This speech mode is one where the structure and syntax are relatively difficult to predict for any one individual and where the formal possibilities of sentence organization are used to clarify meaning and make it explicit. (Bernstein, 1961, p. 291.)

Working-class environments, on the other hand, are characterized by a form of speech that is very direct, unambiguous and closely identified with the speaker. 'It is a form of relatively condensed speech in which certain meanings are restricted and the possibility of their elaboration is reduced' (p. 291). Where the middle-class mother might, for example, say to her child: 'I'd rather you made less noise, darling,' the working-class mother might say: 'Shut up!' But it is not merely the range of words that matter here, but the way they are used. A child growing up in an environment where words are not simply a means of instantly expressed desires or imperatives but of a wide and infinitely complex network of expression, can at an early age become mentally flexible in *his* approach to the world. Life becomes graded into a variety of very fine shades, differing from but allied to one another. The speaker is able to use words like mixing colours on a palette, taking great care to pick those which most closely match his precise meaning. This is not just a matter of a wide vocabulary but of an understanding of the nuances of language.

It is notable that among poorly educated but intelligent people, it is their inability to express themselves precisely enough which leads them, almost in frustration but perhaps inevitably, to talk in absolute terms – and absolute terms breed violence and hatred. Do the roots of racial prejudice lie here, in the first futile struggles with an incoherent form of language that will not permit a sensible resolution of unspoken tensions?

Whatever the answer, it seems fairly clear that in the child's early years the linguistic inheritance he receives may be as much a handicap as a help. For the working class, language that is sufficient for life in a crowded terraced house is not sophisticated enough to cope with the demands that a more formalized school education, for example, makes upon the individual. So a working-class child entering school – itself a middle-class institution stocked with teachers drawn from the middle-classes – not merely begins with a disadvantage, but arrives with social inequality already built into him; an inequality that, although it cannot be avoided entirely, could certainly be ameliorated by the kind of wider social contact that nursery schooling provides, with the encouragement there of the use of language, so often curtailed or sometimes even expressly forbidden in autocratic families.

Chapter Four
The Importance of Play

Play is the highest level of child development. It is the spontaneous expression of thought and feeling – an expression which his inner life requires . . . at this age, play is never trivial; it is serious and deeply significant. It needs to be cherished and encouraged by the parents, for in his free choice of play a child reveals the future life of his mind to anyone who has insight into human nature. The forms of play at this stage are the core of the whole future, since in them the entire person is developed and revealed in the most sensistive qualities of his mind. (Friedrich Froebel, *The Education of Man*.)

Froebel wrote that more than 140 years ago, but it remains true today and has, I think, a particular significance. What we know, or think we know, about children's play – about the significance of phantasy, about aggression and role-play – springs from the work of psychoanalysis, psychologists and psychiatrists. In the last ten years, this area of child development has been looked at again by scientists interested in the biological bases of behaviour. Inevitably, their approach to the problems of the early years of childhood has been very different from the observing and recording techniques of the psychologists, but the evidence is, so far as one can judge at this point in time, that it not merely reinforces and complements the earlier studies, but in every way underpins it. We are not faced with new and conflicting theories, but with added laboratory evidence for the old theories.

What emerges is a sharply etched statement of the importance of play in the development of the young child. Where the conflict really exists is not among the research workers, but in our language itself. Words like 'play' evoke certain value judgements that are equated in the popular mind with 'frivolity', 'irrelevance' and 'inessentials'. Yet in childhood, play is really equivalent to work, and is even more important in the development of the individual personality. Froebel saw this very clearly. In his most famous work, *The Education of Man* he wrote:

Could we but regard our children in the first weeks of their life as inherently sensitive and responsible to their environment how different they and how different mankind would be.... We must escape the decision that insight is denied to the child and that he lacks judgement. True, he wants the adult's power of deductive thought, yet he has a certain spontaneous insight and judgement, an immediate response, which is for that very reason all the more likely to be right. With the smallest child, therefore, we should take particular care to search in his mind for the reality from which all this springs. A baby may appear helpless, but his power of thought is much greater than we imagine.

That seems a remarkable statement to have made more than a century before laboratory evidence was able to confirm that even the youngest child is capable of decided mental effort. Far from the half-blind, tone-deaf bundle of bawling egocentricity that many still assume babies to be, research is showing that even a day-old child is aware of the outside world, of things going on around it.

At Yale University's Child Study Center, for example, three-month-old babies have been given patterns of blinking lights to follow with their eyes, and have memorized them and recorded their pleasure in doing so. Four-month-old children have been put in cribs with mirrors in front of them and with mobiles and moving toys within range of their waving arms and hands. What has been noticed about the enriched environments is not only the pleasure they have given babies, but the added incentive they have given them and the development that has accompanied such stimulus. Learning to blink, a landmark in early child development, has occurred earlier than is normal. So have other features. Dr Burton White of Harvard University has taken a particular interest in the first five months of development and in visually directed reaching – the child seeing an object, wishing to grasp it and directing his arm and hand towards the object and holding it. Most children take some three months to reach this level of sophistication. White, however, has shown that an enriched environment can accelerate this process. Working in a hospital, with babies from the age of six days, he devised a programme of visual stimulus that resulted in his subjects achieving the goal weeks earlier than normal. It is too soon to draw any strong conclusions from such work, but it undoubtedly highlights the importance of play in the development of the child. Dr Jerome Bruner of Harvard has put considerable emphasis on this aspect and believes that the discoveries that are now being made will give the selection of toys for children an added meaning. He is quoted as saying:

Peek-a-boo games are quite extraordinary in their power. They can practically produce cardiac arrest! It's the drama of the object reappearing; is it gone, or not gone? I operate on the assumption that the main source of growth is conflict. This may be an Old Testament view of things, but growth comes from suffering two systems that you can't put together. So this kind of game is the essence of what we have to do.

Perhaps we can design a toy such that if you whack it on one side, it'll go 'ping!', but if you get it on the wrong side, it'll just go 'pfft!' This ought to produce excitement in the child! It would help him to recognize that there are some sequences of behavior that lead somewhere and others that don't.

This whole question of the need for stimulus, which was recognized so early by the pioneers of nursery schooling, is now getting support from the work of psychologists working with animals. Professor Seymour Levine of Stanford University was originally interested in finding out what harmful effect this kind of stimulus might evoke in infancy by giving one batch of young rats mild electric shocks, handling and fondling another group and leaving a third group completely alone. To his great surprise, he found that it was this third group that displayed the unusual, deviant behaviour. Non-manipulated rats, unlike their shocked or fondled counterparts, grew up emotionally immature, were fearful in strange environments, cowered in corners, refused to explore their new world and developed all the accepted reactions to stress.

Under stress, the central nervous system causes the pituitary gland, at the base of the brain, to release larger quantities of various hormones, one of the principal ones being adrenal-corticotrophic hormone (ACTH). Herbert M. Evans of the University of California, one of the greatest modern endocrinologists, carried out research in the twenties on the hormones produced by the pituitary. Since then, the literature on the subject has very considerably increased but a fundamental puzzle remains. It is known that ACTH affects the outer layer of the adrenal glands, and through ACTH the pituitary acts upon these glands and controls them. It is ACTH which appears to alert the adrenal glands to stress conditions causing them to produce an increased amount of other hormones. These, passing through the blood, excite the metabolism of the tissues in such a way that the body remains in balance under the threat of external stress. In other words, there appears to be a sort of circular warning system or, if one prefers, a kind of self-regulating device built into the body. When the stress situation appears, the hypothalamus, which receives outside stimuli signals and might almost be thought of as the radar system of the body, warns the pituitary of stress situations and this sets off the whole chain of events. When the stress passes, it is again the hypothalamus which seems to give the all-clear but, because there are no nervous pathways connecting the hypothalamus to the pituitary, one of the problems facing endocrinologists is how this signalling process works.

Now it may seem that all this endocrinology is far removed from the problems of play in young children, but my theory is that it is fundamental to understanding this activity. What Levine's work showed was that the stimulated animals – and there was no difference between those which had been given shocks and those which had been fondled by humans, itself a rather curious and provocative finding – appeared to have a far more developed stress response. In rats, the adrenal glands begin to function shortly after birth and the pituitary seems to contain ACTH very early in life. The nerve mechanism that controls the release of this hormone, however, does not appear to come into operation until the rat is some sixteen days old. Stimulated rats, however, showed a significant ACTH response as early as twelve days – a difference which, if translated in human terms, would amount to several months. Moreover, this early development was no passing phenomenon. The stimulated rats reached a mature level of resistance to stress considerably earlier because of an accelerated maturation of the central nervous system, confirmed later by an analysis of the brain tissue. And they went on to open their eyes earlier, grow their body hair faster, gain weight more rapidly and in every way behave in a superior fashion to the unstimulated rats.

Dr Levine's important researches (see Levine, 1960) have been repeated with cats, dogs, monkeys and guinea pigs as well as with rats and mice. That is to say, they appear not to be 'culture-limited', although one naturally hesitates to apply findings from laboratory animals to humans. On the other hand, the findings seem to tie in so closely with the work of men like Dr White, and with what we already know about the effects of deprivation in young children, that it seems, to be at least reasonable to suppose that early stimulation – as involved in play – performs a similar function of developing the stress function in children.

Indeed, if this is anywhere near right, it raises important questions about the nature of baby care, and it could be argued that the stimulation affected by mother love – stroking, fondling and playing with the young child – is desirable at the very first stages of life if the maturation processes are to develop to their maximum potentiality. Can we take it further? Can we say that the body itself has a built-in drive to provide such stimulus for itself, and that one of our failings in child rearing is that we have not recognized it for what it is: the factor of curiosity?

All children are curious, almost dangerously so. Why? It is generally held that the basic human drives are hunger, sex, thirst and the alleviation of pain. But if we see curiosity as the drive which produces stimulus, and if this stimulus is necessary to develop fully the central nervous system, then that could be another item to add to the list.

At Wisconsin University, researchers working with monkeys and apes found that the animals were prepared to do puzzles and perform intricate operations for hours on end merely for the reward of looking out of their cages and seeing what was happening in the laboratory. Their curiosity appeared unflagging. One monkey, working almost continuously, opened doors allowing him a view of what was going on outside for nineteen hours at a stretch. What this animal was getting in the way of reward was not food nor any other traditional opiate; it was the satisfaction of his curiosity.

What happens when this basic curiosity drive is not satisfied? William Thompson and Ronald Melzack, two research workers at McGill University, Montreal, tried to answer this using Scottish terriers as their subjects. For the first few months of their lives, these puppies were divided into two groups, one set farmed out and allowed to live normally, the other isolated in private cages, one dog to a cage, out of which they could not see. The isolated dogs lived in these boxes until they were between seven and ten months old. When the caged dogs were released it was found that they behaved in a highly immature way – over-excited, exceptionally playful, less intelligent, agitated at the sight of strange objects, unable to find their way through mazes. One of the most interesting findings was that the restricted dogs behaved as if they were unaware of the source of pain. To the astonishment of the experimenters, these dogs often toyed with the painful stimulus and frequently walked into it. They repeatedly struck their heads against water pipes in the laboratory, and one dog banged his head against these pipes some thirty times in a single hour, without apparently showing any signs of pain.

We were surprised to find that when these dogs grew up they failed to respond normally to a flaming match. Some of them repeatedly poked their noses into the flame and sniffed at it as long as it was present. If they snuffed it out, they reacted similarly to a second flaming match, and even to a third. . . . These dogs also endured pinpricks with little or no evidence of pain. In contrast, littermates that had been reared in a normal environment recognized potential harm so quickly that we were usually unable to touch them with the flame or pin more than once. (R Melzack, 'The perception of pain', *Scientific American*, February 1961.)

What these findings suggest is that there are certain crucial learning areas (critical periods) in the early days of life which, in the case of these particular dogs, had not taken place, and that the central nervous system was not compensating for these. If we recall those other experiments that showed that the development of stress control involved the production of ACTH, and that this could be stimulated by increased activity in the early days of infancy, we could hypothesize that a restriction of stimulus also produces atrophy of the stress mechanisms and that, although this stunting might subsequently be ameliorated, it produces a handicap which, so far as we know, affects the person throughout life.

This is highly unscientific. It does not take into account the purely 'social' stresses bound to arise in groups of confined animals. It takes findings from laboratory animals and translates them into general conclusions about children. The point is, of course, that we cannot lock babies up into wooden boxes so we must search for clues to their development elsewhere. Nor does it matter, here, whether the mechanisms that occur in animals develop in rather different ways in children; it is enough to recognize that play, and the stimulus it affords, is not merely a pleasurable experience, but could well have a fundamental biological role in the developnent of the child.

It has, of course, other important elements as well. Susan Isaacs, who pioneered child development studies virtually single-handed in this country in the twenties, once said that

the chief function of play in the early years is the active dramatization of the inner world of phantasy as a means for maintaining psychic equilibrium. In his play activities, the child externalizes and works out to some measure of harmony all the different trends of his internal psychic life. In turn he gives external form and expression, now to the parent, now to the child, within himself, and to each of the different aspects of his real parents, as he apprehends these at the different levels of his own development, through his own wishes and impulses. And thus gradually he learns to relate his deepest and most primitive phantasies to the ordered world of real experience in time and space.

So when we talk of play we must be careful to differentiate between the satisfaction of curiosity which I believe has a biological source, and the externalizing of mental stress which has a psychological origin. The first leads directly to learning. The second (a sort of conscious dreaming) to understanding and an alleviation of the mental pressures inevitably present in the process of growing up. Both are crucially important for the intellectual and emotional development of the child.

There is, of course, a third factor: the exercising of the motor faculties, which another pioneer, Margaret McMillan, spoke about so eloquently:

Children want space at all ages. But from the age of one to seven, space, that is, ample space, is almost as much wanted as food and air. To move, to run, to find things out by new movement, to 'feel one's life in every limb'; that is the life of early childhood.

What we see, therefore, is that space, the opportunity for imaginative play, the intelligent provision of suitable toys, the facilities for movement and stimulus, are not merely desirable at the pre-school stage; they are essential. But the kind of environment needed for such development is almost exactly the opposite of what we are providing in our communities today. The increased use of tower blocks to house higher densities in urban areas is creating a growing isolation for children at the very time when they need maximum space, companionship, exploration and adventure. The motor car is no friend of the small child. Overtaken by the revolution of the combustion chamber, we have panicked in our attempts to cope with it. But the car has been only an element in the much greater social upheavals that have accompanied it: changing patterns of industrial power, the emancipation of the working classes, the leap from feudalism to democracy. In trying to keep one step ahead of chaos in this whirlwind change, we neglect the true needs of people and build new towns that ignore the young as though they did not exist. We are amazed and affronted when vandalism and anger burst out, and label it juvenile delinquency.

The first recommendation to include a space standard for playgrounds for housing estates did not appear in this country until the Parker–Morris Committee, set up by the Ministry of Housing and Local Government, included it in its report on *Homes for Today and Tomorrow* in 1961. By contrast, it has been a statutory requirement in Copenhagen that play space should be allocated to blocks of flats since the Building Act of 1939.

We still know very little about what is required. The most interesting study of the problem was carried out as long ago as 1959–60, by Dr Vera Hole, who later published her findings in *Research Paper 39* of the National Building Studies 1966. In this study, Dr Hole looked at twelve typical housing estates and found that up to the age of ten, most children were confined to the immediate neighbourhood, however close parks or play centres might be. It was also found that the size of a particular play area was far less important in relation to its use by children than was the equipment provided within it. Furthermore, outdoor play as studied at these areas provided a far more complicated pattern of activity than had been supposed.

The researchers began with a preconception of outdoor play as characteristically quick moving and possibly noisy. Observations soon dispelled this idea. The most frequent activity was sitting, standing or lying down. If to this is added watching and talking, over a third of total activity is of this passive type.

Dr Hole found that even those parents who lived on estates where the provision of play amenities was relatively good were dissatisfied with these provisions, even though local parents were not usually aware of all the possibilities, of facilities which might be provided but were not.

Chapter Five
The Effects of Deprivation

Perhaps the most remarkable fact about the development of the young child is his resilience to external pressures. Forced to endure physical hardship, loss of parents, poor diet, lack of proper medical attention, long illnesses, even wars and concentration camps, children yet emerge, often apparently unimpaired. The urge to survive is a tough, inborn trait. It is not easily defeated.

That this resilience is more apparent than real, however, is now commonly accepted. 'The souls of little children are marvellously delicate and tender things, and keep forever the shadow that first falls on them ...' wrote Olive Schreiner. When we say that the child is tough, what we really mean is that our yardsticks for measuring the impairment of its psychological or physical well-being are crude and open to wide margins of error. Children who smile may be genuinely happy. But they may also be anxious, too ready to please, or simply hiding frustrations and tensions which we are unable to fathom. Children who shout and jump about and clap their hands may be full of fun, or simply immature and overexcitable.

To talk about the deprivation of children is therefore to use a rather loose term. Clinically, the term 'deprivation' is applied to those children who have lost an essential feature of their home environment, such as a mother or a father, or who have no home at all, either because they are abandoned (or are illegitimate offspring with mothers who cannot support them) or because their home has broken up through divorce of the parents or because the parents have been made homeless.

But there are other uses for the term. The most obvious is for the child which grows up on an inadequate diet. The young girls of China who were forced to have their feet bound and were therefore robbed of the opportunity for running about and experiencing the joy of lively movement, could equally be described as deprived in this particular sense. A child who is reared in an atmosphere that is potentially injurious to its health, even if it does not suffer a specific illness, might be said to be deprived. Similarly a child brought up in an environment which is intellectually dull, devoid of stimulus and deadening to the spirit of enquiry might be described as a 'deprived' child.

But to what extent can we measure the degree of deprivation? Is it possible actually to show the effects of such deprivation and, conversely, to indicate the positive virtues of an abundant environment? To do so one has, inevitably, to look at extremes. The most obvious is the example of malnutrition and its effect on intelligence. Workers who have dealt with twins have found that the physically heavier twin at birth is also normally the more intelligent, and that children who are small and puny at birth show signs of mental retardation. Female rats fed on a diet rich in amino acids regularly produce healthy and intelligent litters, but the same rats, when deprived of proteins during pregnancy, give birth to small offspring who perform measurably badly in intelligence tests (Cowley and Griesel, 1966, p. 506).

The point about such deprivation is that it makes its maximum effect upon the very young. If adults are deprived of a proper diet, such as happened in the German concentration camps during the last war, there does not appear to be any lasting effect on them once their health has been restored. As far as their intelligence is concerned, there does not seem to be any decrease as a result of starvation. With children, however, a poor diet would seem to have quiet marked affects not only upon their physical development, but also on their mental growth.

This is not surprising. In the case of a child's height, for example, we know that while the general pattern is governed by genetic factors, environment can cause a considerable deviation in the end figure. It has been suggested that the difference between children who grow up in rich environments and those brought up in poor ones can be as great as 10 per cent. That is to say, an abundant environment can increase the potential height of a child by 5 per cent, while a bad environment can stunt the potential by 5 per cent. This creates a vast difference. It means that for two children genetically endowed to grow to 5 ft 10 in, one might be encouraged to grow to 6 ft 1½ in and another, from a poor background, might only reach 5 ft 6½ in – a difference of seven inches for two children who began with the same potential.

But we already know that the development we are discussing does not take place evenly throughout a child's life and, moreover, that any one stage of development is irreversible. It is therefore obvious that if the environment is poor during the stages when the development is greatest, it will have a much more marked effect upon the final adult than if it is poor during a period when the development is itself only making small progress.

It has been estimated by Bloom (1964) that the differences between a deficient and an abundant environment can result in a variation in height as great as 5·4 per cent if the deprivation takes place in the first three years of life. If this difference is present during the next nine years of life, it will only result in a 3·2 per cent variation. So while it might be correct to say that two children, growing up in different surroundings, might end up with a 10 per cent difference in height, we can see that if these different surroundings are present for only the first three years of their lives, the damage is already extensive and accounts for more than half of the final variation.

Working with identical twins, researchers have found that differences of environment also affect a child's intelligence. In extreme cases – that is where one of the children is brought up in an abundant environment and the other in a very bad one – they have recorded differences of about twenty I.Q. points in children who would normally have developed the same I.Q. Taking this figure, Bloom (1964, p. 72) has constructed a table that combines the development curve of the human intelligence with the effects of deprivation.

Table 1
Hypothetical Effects of Different Environments on the
Development of Intelligence in Three Selected Age Periods

Variation from Normal Growth in I.Q. units

Age period	Per cent of mature intelligence	Deprived	Normal	Abundant	Abundant-deprived
Birth–4	50	−5	0	+5	10
4–8	30	−3	0	+3	6
8–17	20	−2	0	+2	4
Total	100	−10	0	+10	20

What this table shows is the far greater effects of deprivation in the first four years of life than in subsequent stages of development, for the simple reason that it is in these early years that the intelligence is itself advancing most rapidly.

But what is it about these environments that we keep describing as abundant or deprived? Is it sunlight or proteins, a clean home or the opportunity for conversation? It is, of course, all of these things. But one of the most crucial factors is an environment in which the growing child is loved and in which it is able to make a particular attachment to one person, normally the mother. In order for a child to develop mentally it needs stability in its early years, the particular stability that a well-organized home, supported by both parents can provide and in which the mother takes an active and personal interest in the child.

The importance of this factor has been amply demonstrated by a survey prepared by Dr John Bowlby (1964) for the World Health Organisation. In this study, Dr Bowlby quoted the experiment carried out by a New York psychologist, Dr W. Goldfarb. The object of this experiment was to show how the personality of children was affected when they were brought up in the highly impersonal surroundings of an institution instead of the richly personal one of a home. What Dr Goldfarb did was to compare the mental development of children brought up until the age of three in an institution and afterwards placed in foster-homes, with that of other children who had gone into foster-homes immediately after birth.

The two groups of children had similar heredities, and fifteen pairs of children were most carefully matched, so that any differences that arose could with confidence be ascribed to their different upbringing. In fact, the group of children who went into institutions came from mothers whose occupational, educational and mental standing was, if anything, slightly superior to those whose children went directly into foster-homes. Moreover, the foster-homes themselves were scrupulously matched, so that any differences due to the later environment were avoided.

The institutions to which half the children went were themselves very clean places, but they lacked human contact or stimulus. Babies below the age of nine months were each kept in their own little cubicles to prevent the spread of epidemic infection and their only contact with adults occurred during a few hurried moments in the day when they were dressed, changed or fed by nurses. Later, the children were gathered in groups of fifteen or twenty under the supervision of one nurse, who had neither the training nor the time to offer them affection or attention. As a result they lived in 'almost complete social isolation during the first years of their life' and their experience in the succeeding two years was only slightly better.

The two groups were studied by a great variety of tests. In intelligence, in power of abstract thinking, in their social maturity, their power of keeping rules and making friends, the institution group fell far below those who had stayed with their foster-parents throughout their early years. Only three of the fifteen children from the institution were up to the average in speech, while all fifteen of the children from the foster-homes reached this level. It is worth remembering that in this particular experiment, both sets of children had suffered deprivation of some sort in that neither had enjoyed an ordinary home with natural parents looking after them. But despite this, the differences between the two groups was vast.

Of course, research of this kind tends to deal with very special cases and while the studies allow us to make some fairly general conclusions about all children, we must remember that the great majority of children do not go into special institutions or become the victims of what are called 'broken homes'. Similarly, while the degree of deprivation among children from these kind of homes, or from those where a father is permanently missing, is clear and open to measurement, other, more subtle, kinds of deprivation are much harder to measure.

Dr Bowlby drew certain conclusions from the evidence. He suggested (1964, pp. 60–61) that

if mental development is to proceed smoothly, it would appear to be necessary for the unformed mentality to be exposed, during certain critical periods, to the influence of a psychic organizer – the mother. For this reason, in considering the disorders to which personality and conscience are liable, it is imperative to have regard to the phases of development of the child's capacity for human relationships. These are many, and naturally merge into one another. In broad outline, the following are the most important:

(a) The phase during which the infant is in course of establishing a relation with a clearly defined person – his mother; this is normally achieved by five or six months of age.

(b) The phase during which he needs her as an ever-present companion. This usually continues until about his third birthday.

(c) The phase during which he is becoming able to maintain a relationship with her in her absence. During the fourth and fifth years such a relationship can only be maintained in favourable circumstances and for a few days or weeks at a time; after seven or eight the relationship can be maintained, though not without strain, for periods of a year or more.

The Goldfarb experiment showed up most clearly the handicap that institutionalized children suffer in their speech development, probably the most critical feature concerned with the growth of intelligence.

In another study, a special point was made of investigating this aspect and of measuring the differences, if any, in speech development in pre-school children living in residential care and those living with their own families. Thirty-six children, eighteen from a nursery school and a further eighteen from different residential nurseries, were involved in the experiment (Pringle and Tanner, 1965). As always, the children were carefully matched, for age, sex, intelligence and home background. What the researchers wanted to find out about these children was how they used formal language and the extent of their vocabularies when used in both spontaneous and controlled conditions. They were given both tests and interviews and observed when they were freely playing among themselves. They were shown pictures and asked to comment on them, asked simple questions and had their conversations recorded.

'Wherever quantitative comparison was possible, the nursery school children were found to be in advance of the children in residential nurseries' was the conclusion reached by the researchers.

In conversation, the nursery school group used a wider vocabulary, showed rather better descriptive powers and a more mature type of sentence formation. On the other hand, there was little difference between the two groups in their use of the main grammatical components of speech; many definitions were given in similar terms and both groups tended to find the same words difficult to explain. Thus it seems that although the residential nursery children were retarded in the formal aspects of language, their speech was nevertheless developing along normal lines. (Pringle and Tanner, 1965, p. 132.)

Strangely enough, the kind of comparative studies we have been discussing are very old in origin. In Plutarch's *Lives*, Lycurgus, the lawgiver of the Spartans, took newborn puppies from a litter and brought them up in different environments. 'Men of Sparta, of a truth, habit and training and teaching and guidance in living are a great influence towards engendering excellence, and I will make this evident to you at once,' he said, showing off the different dogs with their various characteristics shaped by their different upbringing. But the Spartans did not learn from him; neither have we.

We have already seen the special concern that the Plowden Committee showed about the deprivation suffered by young children living in poor areas, where the resources do not exist for the stimulation of the child and in which his health might be impaired. But sometimes this kind of cultural deprivation can take more subtle forms. The 'sober little charge' whose parents were both university lecturers and who left their daughter in the charge of a nanny, who in turn considered a television programme to be the highlight of their day, might, in perhaps a different way, be considered equally deprived.

These kinds of children, who fall under no easily defined category and whose particular hardship is often difficult to uncover, have been described by Sir Alec Clegg, Chief Education Officer of the West Riding, as 'twilight children'.

I refer to those children who are wretched and distressed almost beyond endurance because of what they suffer in their homes, and may I stress that I do not necessarily mean homes which are poverty-stricken or neglected homes which for any reason might come within the purview of the police, or homes which fall exclusively into any one class. Cruelty knows no social barriers and may be all the more poignant if refined by education. Broken homes occur right throughout society. (*Where?* March 1966, p. 19.)

The kind of child he had in mind was the product of a home which, although it was not officially 'broken', contained parents who did not speak to one another, or had a father earning £16 who only gave £2 to his wife and openly kept another woman with the rest; the father who never worked; the mother not 'mental' enough to be certified but who followed her child to school and shouted down the corridors.

Sir Alec Clegg, who carried out a survey of 190 schools to find out the kind of hardship that existed, found a second category of children suffering from 'social disease', the children of fathers with notorious tempers and fits of brutality, or of mothers who are weak and vacillating, or with a parent who is mentally handicapped.

The whole problem is aggravated by a point of view which is valid enough when applied to certain forms of distress but deplorable in its effect when applied to others. It has been realized that the affection of the home is a powerful force in achieving for a child the security and well-being which he needs. It has also been realized that if a child has to live with poverty or squalor or even what we call immorality, he may, nevertheless, get the affection which he needs. But it is surely the height of stupidity to allow his faith in the home to become so blind that a child is made to live in circumstances where he is not only bereft of love but even constantly faced with fear or even hate.

The kind of studies we have been looking at are, of course, concerned with children 'deprived' in the most extreme use of the term, in which they have been compared with children who, if not in normal households, have at least enjoyed a reasonable environment.

What is impossible to study is the differences that might exist between children in what Bloom has termed 'abundant' environments and those in normal homes. In Bloom's calculations of the maximum deviation in I.Q. between children in various extreme environments, much weight has been given to the measurements made of identical twins reared in different homes. As a scientist, Professor Bloom has naturally avoided the temptation to look beyond the available evidence, but the question must be asked as to whether even these figures present a true picture of what is possible if a super-abundant environment could be provided for the pre-school child.

In most of the literature on the pre-school child, for example, research workers have taken it for granted that a stable home environment, complete with a mother who loves the child, a father who provides support for the mother and the financial resources for a sound diet, a lively atmosphere and the possibilities of a variety of pre-school experiences – holidays, outings, books, picnics – is in itself the definition of a rich environment. Certain other factors need to be taken into account: the health of the mother, the number of other children in the home, the amount of space available for the child, the attitude of the parents towards the free movement of the child, the degree to which the parents are prepared to make their home a child-centred one, the amount of time devoted to playing and to talking to the child, the cultural level of the parents themselves, and the opportunities available for the pre-school child to mingle with other children and socialize with them. Are there pets in the family? Is the home situated on a busy street, and if it is, is there a garden large enough for the child to run in, and does it have trees for the child to climb in? Is there room for a sandpit and a climbing frame, or a rope ladder? Does the child get the opportunity to work with different materials, such as wood, or soft metal, or plastics? Is the mother house-proud to a degree where the child is circumscribed in his movements and activities? Is the father more concerned about his carefully tended rose bushes than about the needs of his child? Does the family allow the child to have a play-room, or a bedroom large enough for him to spread his toys about and play imaginative games? Are there opportunities for the child to hear and appreciate good music, or is the home filled with pop music from morning till night?

All these questions, and a hundred more, might come into an assessment as to whether a home provides a rich environment for the pre-school child or not, and it might be argued that if any of these requirements were not met then, to that degree, the child was deprived of so much opportunity for experience and experimentation. What we are not in a position to measure at present is the extent to which a truly enriched environment of the kind I have suggested might still further extend the amount by which the final I.Q. of any child might deviate from its genetic endowment. What seems almost certain is that Bloom's standard twenty points will be extended still further and that one day, when enlightenment has taken us a little further, 'deprivation' will come to mean not merely the absence of the crude essentials of young life, but the denial of those more subtle encouragements and opportunities that the eager young mind craves.

It is, however, only reasonable that in our present state of knowledge, attention should be focused on those children who do not enjoy even the fundamental rights of childhood. Certainly it was these children who attracted the notice of those pioneers who many years ago fought so hard to improve their lot. The question we must ask about their efforts today is: how is it that they failed to get their message accepted?

Chapter Six
The Early Pioneers

It was, of course, the deprivation, squalor, hardship and suffering that accompanied the Industrial Revolution in Europe that first attracted reformers to the needs of the child, just as today it is the plight of the depressed areas that draws the attention of the Plowden Committee. And rightly so. But it is perhaps unfortunate that the idea of nursery education has become so inevitably associated in the public mind with rescue work and overlaid with emphasis on remedial treatment, for it has made harder the task of convincing society as a whole that the early years of any child are too important to be left unattended.

It was the plight of children left to their own resources while their mothers worked in the fields that inspired a Protestant pastor, Johann Friedrich Oberlin, to begin the first nursery in the village of Waldbach in Alsace, in 1799. The actual idea for the scheme seems to have come from Oberlin's maidservant, Louise Scheppler, a formidable woman who actually ran the school until her death in 1837. But it was Oberlin who inspired it, just as he did the 'knitting school' for older children in the same village, where they were taught to sew and were read stories. Oberlin developed a corpus of ideas about the education of young people, and his liberal views had a great influence on later developments in Germany. But his main contribution will always be seen as a provider for the young and the founder of the nursery school movement. The experiment in that small village created much interest throughout the country. Early in the nineteenth century, a somewhat similar venture – this time for children up to four years of age – was started in Detmold, in Germany, and from then on the nursery school movement began to spread throughout Europe. A M. Firmin Marbeau began the first *crèche* in Paris in November 1844, again for the benefit of children whose mothers went out to work. It was not intended to be free, but designed to help those mothers who were obliged actually to leave their houses in search of work.

The Germans introduced a rather similar scheme with their *Bewahranstalten*, and these nurseries, together with the German *Krippe* (the equivalent of the French *crèche*) were opened throughout the country. In 1869 the French government gave official recognition to the *crèche* movement and by the end of the century there were sixty-eight *crèches* in Paris itself, another forty-four in the suburbs and 322 in other departments. The Belgians, too, adopted the idea of providing official areas where working mothers could leave their small children, and in their case called them *jardins des enfants*. Austria was more impressed with the work of Froebel, who had opened the first kindergarten in 1837 and had, furthermore, established the first training college for kindergarten teachers. The Austrians decided to adopt the Froebel philosophy to the extent of a decree passed by their Ministry of Education in 1872, recognizing kindergartens as part of the country's education system.

What we see throughout the nineteenth century in Europe, therefore, is a ferment of ideas, of quick development and of official recognition for the world of the young child, and by 1908 it was possible to say that half the children between two and five in Belgium, a quarter of those in France and between 2 and 10 per cent in Germany were regularly attending institutions of some kind.

The ideas of men like Oberlin, Pestalozzi and Froebel also made their way across the Channel to England. But here official views held that far fewer women went out to work than on the Continent, and that therefore no special provisions were necessary. Hardly concerned about the work of Robert Owen, officialdom was even less likely to be stirred by the preachings of foreigners.

Owen's biographer, the Socialist thinker G. D. H. Cole, described him as 'a puzzle' and 'a little mad' (Owen, 1927, introduction). What certainly seems awesome about both his life and beliefs today is that both were so clearly out of tune with the society of the time. He was born into the most turbulent period of the Industrial Revolution, in a little village in Montgomeryshire in central Wales. His father was a local saddler and ironmonger, and also acted as the postmaster. A bright child, the young Robert Owen became a sort of pupil-teacher in his own school at the age of seven and by nine had left to take employment at the village shop. Then he left the area, to travel to Lincolnshire, to London for a brief stay and finally to Manchester; the Manchester of Engels, that was growing in wealth upon the inventions of men like Hargreaves, Arkwright and Crompton, and where fortunes were being made out of their new processes for the cotton industry. Owen himself became the owner, for a short time, of a mill, but was soon offered the job of manager of one of the largest and best equipped spinning mills in Lancashire. From there he moved, at the age of twenty-eight, to take charge of the famous New Lanark Mills, the biggest in Scotland. It was a brilliant rise.

Horrified by what he had seen of the processes of industry and the way the new manufacturing techniques were turning men into machines, to be worked night and day until the last commercial penny had been wrung out of them, Owen now set himself to create, not a factory, but a new type of community. New Lanark became his test-tube for Socialism.

'The rich wallow in an excess of luxuries injurious to themselves, solely by the labour of men who are debarred from acquiring for the own use and sufficiency even of the indispensible articles of life,' he wrote to the Earl of Liverpool, determined to instigate factory reforms and use the newly acquired wealth of industry for the betterment of the people who made it work (Owen, 1927, p. 133). At New Lanark he set about breaking every managerial code that at the time was considered essential for the proper running of a business. He refused, for example, to employ any children in his mills under the age of ten, when most mill-owners were employing, for virtually no salary, boys under six.

Instead of children being admitted at nine years of age to work in cotton mills twelve and a half hours a day, with only an hour and a half for meals and recreation, no child should be admitted to work in any manufactory before ten years of age and not for more than six hours per day until he is twelve years old. (Owen, 1927, p. 137.)

He insisted on paying his workers high wages at a time when owners believed that it was only by paying the bare minimum that profits could be made. He had homes built for them, and considered their welfare an essential duty for any manager. And despite the ridicule of his contemporaries, Owen's mills made profits, pointing the way to the 'economics of high wages' which has supplanted the policy of sweated labour so universal in his time.

Owen did many things during his life. He was, basically, the father of Socialism, of trades unionism, and the originator of two social communities, one in America and one in England, both of which foundered. He instigated factory reform and was an inveterate writer and pamphleteer. But one of his most notable achievements occurred in 1816, when he stood up in a building in New Lanark to open what he called the Institution for the Formation of Character. He told his mill workers on that day:

The Institution has been devised to afford the means of receiving your children at an early age, as soon almost as they can walk. By this means many of you, mothers of families, will be able to earn a better maintenance or support for your children; you will have less care and anxiety about them; while the children will be prevented from acquiring any bad habits, and gradually prepared to learn the best. (Owen, 1927, p. 98.)

What was remarkable about this particular reform was not merely that he saw so clearly what was required in the social circumstances of his day, but could move so far ahead of even the educators in his approach to children's learning.

The children were not to be annoyed with books: but were to be taught the uses and nature and qualities of the common things around them by familiar conversation when the children's curiosity was excited, so as to induce them to ask questions respecting them.

One would hardly argue with that even today.

But Robert Owen was a lonely voice in an England convulsed with a search for power and quick wealth. Nobody took up the challenge he threw out about social responsibilities and for almost a century the needs of young children were, except by a few isolated enthusiasts, ignored. One of the reasons for this was that a tradition had arisen in England that if the parents so desired, children between three and five years of age could attend elementary school classes, where provision was made to take these children. When a consultative committee looked into the matter in 1908, it found that at least a third of all the children in England between the ages of three and five were on the registers of these elementary schools.

It was, of course, not educationally desirable that these very young children should be lumped together with the older ones in this way and soon, after the passing of the Education Act of 1902, some of the newly established local education authorities began to take the matter seriously. For the elementary schools were run along the most rigid lines, with formal seating at desks, strong doses of rote learning and a heavy-handed approach to the serious business of reading, writing and arithmetic. The buildings were sombre, the classes averaged sixty or seventy children, and the teaching was imbued with all the humourless severity of the dying Victorian era.

In 1905 the then Board of Education published the reports of five women inspectors on the position of children under five in public elementary schools, and as a result of their recommendations the following words were introduced into the regulations:

Where the Local Education Authority have so determined in the case of any school maintained by them, children who are under five years of age may be refused admission to that school.

The view of the women inspectorate was that, because the elementary school classes were obviously inappropriate for young children, special provision ought to be made for them in their own nursery schools. They recommended that, with these facilities provided, the under-fives should then be kept out of the crowded, badly lit and badly ventilated elementary schools. But the regulations made no mention of nursery school provision and the Board of Education, in its 1905 Code, gave complete discretion in the matter to the local authorities, without in any way stipulating that the change was dependent on alternative arrangements being made. The result of this change of procedure is easily seen in the statistics. In 1900, there were 622,498 under-fives attending school out of a total throughout the country of some 1,435,605: some 43 per cent. By 1926 the actual number attending was 181,492, out of an estimated under-five population of 1,413,217: down to 13 per cent.

This incredible chapter in the history of English education, inexplicable as it now seems, took place, moreover, in a society where infant mortality stood at about 160 deaths per 1000, and in which the conditions of life seriously stunted the development of possibly one in three members of the population. That, at any rate, was the proportion of men who, examined by the army for service in the Boer War, were rejected by the medical officers as unfit for military service.

Between 1893 and 1902 some 35 per cent of the recruits considered for war service were rejected upon initial inspection, another 1 per cent were rejected within three months of inspection, and a further 2 per cent were dismissed during their first year in the army, according to the *Report on Physical Deterioration* published in 1904. But even these very high figures do not give a true picture of the effects that over-crowding, malnutrition, poor hygiene, disease and the ravages of poverty had upon the population. It was estimated that of the 77 per cent of the nation living in towns, perhaps a quarter – or about six million people – were living in actual poverty. If this factor was taken into account, it might, according to Sir Frederick Maurice, the Inspector-General of Recruiting at the time, mean that as many as 60 per cent of the nation's potentially recruitable males were unable to meet the modest requirements of the army.

It was the sight of children straying 'half naked, unwashed, and covered in sores' through the filthy streets of the East End of London at this time which inspired the sisters Rachel and Margaret McMillan to devote their considerable energies to remedial work among infants. They were a remarkable couple.

Since 1895, Rachel had worked as a travelling teacher of hygiene among the villagers of Kent. She knew all about the poor, and the apathy and squalor that poverty breeds. 'In many ways,' she once said, 'the cottage girls do not grow up. They remain always at the age of twelve or thirteen. The grown women do not merely write like children; in many ways they think like children' (McMillan, 1927a, p. 92).

Margaret, as a member of the board of Bradford School, was equally appalled at the sight of children 'in every stage of illness. Children with adenoids. Children with curvature. Children in every state of neglect and dirt and suffering.' Together these sisters, who every Sunday morning sold their Christian Socialist tracts along the docklands of the East End, set about to change the position. As members of the Independent Labour Movement they were already crusaders for 'a new system in which co-operation and the creation of wealth for use would take the place of mere scrambling for power and existence.' Now they set out to harness their considerable political fervour and reformist zeal to ameliorate the life of the children whom Rachel McMillan saw as she made her way from Kent to the Greenwich Observatory, where she went to stare in fascination at the astronomical instruments kept there.

The two sisters drafted plans for 'a place of healing in schools' and approached the Board of Education. Sir Robert Morant, one of the most famous of the administrators of the education system at the turn of the century, was sympathetic and offered the support of his school inspectors. More helpful still was the sudden and unexpected support of an impulsive, cause-conscious American soap millionaire, Joseph Fels, who turned up with £5000. With this money and with at least the tacit support of the authorities, the McMillan sisters opened the first school clinic in Bow in 1908. It was their belief that a centre where children could be treated for some of the more chronic ailments would be welcomed by the people of the area. But instead, the clinic was treated with suspicion and fear, and although the children who came were successfully treated, the small numbers who used the clinic made the cost of each case prohibitive. By March 1910 the Bow clinic was closed and another in Deptford was opened. This one was very much more successful. It had more money, more general support from the authorities and a special committee to run it. Six thousand children a year crowded in at lunch hours and after four o'clock to see the resident doctor and dentist. Because both sisters were struck by the appalling incidence of tonsillitis and adenoidal infection among the children, an operation centre was opened near by, and twenty children came each Saturday to have their tonsils and adenoids removed, Rachel staying with them to provide comfort and help.

The work of these pioneering women did not go unnoticed. A dental grant was offered to the centre in 1911 and a further grant to help with the medical work was given the following year. By that time a near-by garden had already been converted into a camp for the children, to give them an opportunity to escape from the claustrophobic, unventilated and polluted atmospheres of their homes. What the sisters wanted to provide was fresh air, light and space. They put up canvas awnings over fixed gas pipes and turned an outside drain into a shower bath. More canvas was turned into camp beds, and in this improvised camp seventeen girls spent a whole year sleeping in the open without a single one of them catching pneumonia.

A neighbouring churchyard, belonging to the church of St Nicholas, was now turned into an equivalent camp for boys, who cheerfully snuggled down between the crosses and the monuments as the McMillans seized upon every open space they could find. A piece of waste land became the site for their first proper shelter, and with the help of volunteers, some forty boys and fifteen girls were put up full-time in its temporary huts.

The two sisters rushed about on their rescue missions, dragging children out of their dark, sodden and crowded houses and trying, in every way they could, to remedy the deleterious effects of disease and malnutrition. But to Rachel McMillan, at least, the remedial aspects of her work, while they dominated her life, were not the most important aspect of her mission.

The injury done to the child of poor streets and slums is not to be remedied by any form of literary or secondary education.

New environment, and a new study of organic subjects involving the speech centres, the middle brain and the respiratory and circulatory systems – these must come first. These won, it is possible to build a new structure, to aim at a wider education, to attempt the unfolding of a new personality. (McMillan, 1927a, p. 128.)

It was this wider aim that really inspired Rachel McMillan and led her to begin an open-air nursery school in the tiny gardens of Evelyn House in Deptford in 1913. To this school came six children under the age of five, though the number was soon increased to thirty.

In front of the school, there is a low fence and gateway, over which robust little people can climb without danger and over which all – weak and strong – can watch the movement of life in the garden and can also see the gate through which mother will come and take them home. . . . It is not only air that stagnates indoors. . . . If one cannot at all times see the world that is moving, living, changing, there are sure to be inner restraints and fears. (McMillan, 1927a, p. 142.)

The school prospered. It was enlarged, and had facilities added for the training of child welfare officers and infant teachers. By 1927 the number of children who went there had increased to 230, 80 per cent of whom arrived suffering from some degree of rickets. It was the proud claim of the school, substantiated by the records, that after three years in this nursery, only 7 per cent of these children, who would otherwise have been condemned to a life of ill health and severe handicap, were still unfit for the elementary schools by the time they were five.

But Margaret McMillan saw this as no more than the school's most urgent work.

Is its most startling effect that every rickety child is cured within a year? No. The finest results of the open air schools are mental, not physical. They are found in the rapid progress of alert and awakened children who learn in a few weeks what, under other conditions, they might have spent years trying to acquire. All this is undeniable. It is proved beyond dispute.

The work of the McMillan sisters was crucial to the whole question of provision for the under-fives, but the official position remained ambiguous, as it does to the present day.

In 1907 the consultative committee to the Board of Education was asked to consider the need for making some provision for infants whose home conditions were imperfect, the possible methods of dealing with these children, the ideal institution for them, and the advantages to be derived from attendance at such institutions, to be called nursery schools. The committee, which heard a great deal of evidence, came out with the view that although it felt the ideal place for a child under five was in the home, the economic and social conditions of large numbers of children were such that special nursery schools were the best for them. As a rule, said the committee, such schools should be attached to the public elementary schools. 'The ideal institution for young infants will, as a rule, form an integral part of the Public Elementary Schools system.'

Now these recommendations were important, not only because they stressed that the education of very young children should be divorced from the rigid and formal teaching in the elementary schools, but because they put on record the view that children from two to five (one-third of whom were then at elementary schools) ought to have places of their own, but within the national system as part of the whole.

The outcome of these findings was, however, inertia, and the result was that children who had been enrolled at the elementary schools declined enormously. By 1916 Sir George Newman, the Chief Medical Officer to the Board of Education, recommended yet again that special provisions should be made for the nursery-school child. He advocated that the age period for the nursery school should be widened from three to perhaps five or six years.

Eventually, it might be thought desirable that all little children should be educated on the lines now suggested for Nursery Schools, but that time is not yet come, and further experiment and experience would be needed before any general conclusion could be arrived at.

In the Education Act of 1918, Section 18 empowered local authorities to make arrangements for

supplying or aiding the supply of Nursery Schools for children over two and under five years of age or such later age as may be approved by the Board of Education, whose attendance at such is necessary or desirable for their healthy physical and mental development; and attending to the health, nourishment and physical welfare of children attending Nursery Schools.

It also recommended that

notwithstanding the provisions of any Act of Parliament, the Board of Education may, out of moneys provided by Parliament, pay grants in aid of Nursery Schools, provided that such grants shall not be paid in respect of any such school unless it is open to inspection by the Local Education Authority and unless that Authority is enabled to appoint representatives on the body of managers to the extent of at least one-third of the total number of managers.

Unfortunately, this Act, while it gave recognition to the separate work and identity of the nursery school, also did something more. It caused administrators to think of the pre-school child as a special case, a sort of lonely waif in need of a kind of attention quite different from that provided for a five- or six-year-old. The result was that by 1921 an anomaly had been created within the Education Act of that year, whereby the nursery school was classed as a special school, out of the mainstream of the normal educative process and the education structure. The 1918 Act provided that, in areas where proper provision had been made for nursery education, parents need not be required to send their children to the elementary school until they were six. The idea was good, and was based directly on the views of the Chief Medical Officer. But the result was that the elementary schools were able to close their doors to more young children, and nursery schools were, by and large, not provided. By 1928 there were only twenty-six of them throughout the country, eleven established by local authorities and fifteen by voluntary committees, with a total accommodation for 1367 children, in a year when there were 1,413,217 qualified to attend them.

There is an extraordinary parallel between this situation and some of the recommendations of the 1967 Plowden Committee Report. For in that Report, the suggestion is made that, dependent upon the provision of nursery schools, local authorities might slightly raise the age of entry to infant schools to an average of five years six months. Once again, a well-meaning public body has gone on record with the idea that children can be kept out of the state education system, just as long as nursery schools are provided. But this was exactly the view of the consultative committee of 1905 and the shapers of the 1918 Education Act, and in both cases, the result was that nursery education was not provided and that doors were closed to young children by the national system.

Margaret McMillan was quite certain of what could be achieved if the nation did its duty.

The Nursery School should make a new Junior School possible, because it will send out children who are equipped for a much easier and more rapid advance than is the average child of today. ... The modern world of interest and movement and wonder will be ajar for him already.

In short, if it is a real place of nurture, and not merely a place where babies are 'minded' till they are five, it will affect our whole educational system very powerfully and very rapidly.

The Bastilles will fall at last – by the touch of a little hand. (McMillan, 1927b, pp. 93 and 95.)

Chapter Seven
Social Needs and Social Neglect

The Bastilles of officialdom proved, despite all Margaret McMillan's optimism, to be very durable.

In 1928, a special committee whose job it was to look at various problems within the education system in England turned its attention to nursery schooling.

There is still a widespread unwillingness to regard the needs of children under five as constituting an educational problem at all. We believe that in the light of what is being done in the places – so lamentably few, considering what might be accomplished – where they are systematically provided for, this attitude is demonstrably wrong. If it is wrong, we claim that the plea for the Nursery School ought to be irresistible, and that we ought not to rest until it has found – not merely here and there where some crying necessity is too obvious to be ignored, but everywhere – a recognized placed in our educational system. (*The Case for Nursery Schools*, 1929.)

This was not a propaganda statement by a group with a vested interest in nursery schooling. Its members included Percy Nunn, head of a London teachers' training college who was to become Professor of Education at London University, R. H. Tawney, A. Mansbridge and Freda Hawtry. Two years earlier, this same committee had produced another report, *The Next Step in National Education*, which had advocated the improvement of secondary schooling.

The committee in its report (*The Case for Nursery Schools*, 1929) revealed that of the 3,403,602 children under school age, only some 186,000 were at that time receiving any kind of educational attention, the vast majority of them in the elementary schools.

About three million children are outside the purview of any institution for education and nurture, and it is probable that very many of them come under no medical supervision whatever. If attention be restricted to those between the ages of two and five, the number is almost two million. These constitute a sufficiently serious problem. (ibid., p. 36.)

What made the position in 1928 seem rather better than it actually was was the residual habit of some authorities of accepting children on the elementary school roll. In London, Leeds and some other major centres, young children were still taken in if accommodation was available for them, and in 1926 there were still 181,500 small children attending these schools. The majority of authorities, however, had stopped taking them and another forty-four authorities had less than twenty in any one of their schools. Reorganization of schools was constantly decreasing the amount of accommodation available for the under-fives, and there was an active decline in the number of these children attending any sort of school.

The committee was emphatic about its findings:

It used to be the custom to take a child and ask the question: 'What will he become?' To impress on the minds of others how great were the possibilities of the child, pictorial representations were furnished showing the various stages both of an upward and a downward progress. The implied moral was that, in the main, personal care or neglect might lead to one or other result. It is necessary to discuss whether the picture conveyed the whole truth. Life is complicated, and the currents and cross-currents are so strong and so confusing that it is difficult to portray in so simple a manner all the factors that control development.

But one truth at least is vividly suggested by this picture. It is the importance of the child, and the value to the community and to itself of its proper care and training. This view of the child's importance has secured progressive support during the last quarter of a century from all alike who interest themselves in education or in social reform. ... The whole future of the young child and of the nation may largely depend on the first seven years. This rediscovery of the child and his supreme value to the State characterizes the thought and outlook of the educators of the present age, and may provide a solution for some of our gravest problems. (ibid., pp. 49–50.)

The committee was also quite clear about its conclusions:

The natural thing would be to regard the whole school period before seven – that is, from the age of two or three to seven – as the first or infants' stage, the period from seven to eleven as the primary stage, and that from eleven onwards as the post-primary. (ibid., p. 110.)

This was a remarkably prescient view, for it anticipated by some forty years, an experiment like the Eveline Lowe School in Camberwell, where this very suggestion has been adopted (see Chapter Seven). But 1929 was not a very good time for making suggestions about spending money, however sensible their basis. Nothing was done. In 1942 the Ministry of Education and the Ministry of Health brought out a joint publication called *Not Yet Five* aimed at introducing the work of the nurseries to young people who might like to work in them. In this was included the hopeful sentiment that 'in the years ahead we may expect to see an extension of these more flexible arrangements' (p. 20). But still nothing was done.

To those who saw the education of the very young as one of the keystones of the entire social system, the writing of the 1944 Education Act was a ray of hope. The new Department of Education, under Section 8(2)(b) of that Act, gave local authorities the power 'for securing that provision is made for pupils who have not attained the age of five years by the provision of nursery schools ... or nursery classes in other schools.' During the war the Ministry of Health encouraged local authorities to open day nurseries to free mothers for work in the factories. Thousands of such day nurseries were created. When the war ended, and again on the assumption that there was to be a full-scale plan for nursery schooling, the Ministry began to dismantle the entire apparatus. According to a Ministry of Health circular,

the right policy to pursue would be positively to discourage mothers of children under two from going to work; to make provision for children between two and five by way of nursery schools and classes; and to regard day nurseries and daily guardians as supplements to meet the special needs ... of children whose mothers are incapable for some good reason of undertaking the full care of their children. (Ministry of Health Circular 221/45.)

In 1946 the Ministry of Health ended its 100 per cent grants to local authorities for the opening of day nurseries, which at that time were providing accommodation for some 71,806 children. The result was a steady decline in their provision. By 1964 there were only about 450 day nurseries in the country, providing places for about 21,530 children.

The Ministry of Health was also given a role in the provision for young children by the Nurseries and Child Minders Regulation Act of 1948, under which it was made responsible for the registration and supervision of private nurseries as well as the homes of those who, for a fee, look after more than two children under five years of age. This piece of legislation was made necessary by the increasing problem of the shortage of facilities for young children whose mothers went out to work. Because of a lack of national policy, individuals set themselves up as 'child-minders' and in some cases kept children in appalling conditions for disproportionately high fees. Some control was needed, but even now this is insufficient, and it has not proved feasible to stamp out completely the practice of some private child-minders who are tempted to take more children than their homes can reasonably accommodate. Here is a reported example:

A woman was minding half-a-dozen babies in one small stuffy room with an oil heater. She went out to take another child to school, leaving the man she lived with in charge. He had come off night shift and went to bed. A crawling baby overturned the oil heater and one baby burned to death. Until this happened, the Council did not know she was 'looking after' children, though she claimed to mothers that she was licenced and was charging 25s. a week per child. (*Kilburn Times*, 31 January 1964, quoted in Howe, 1966, p. 31.)

In the face of a growing social need and an increased awareness by parents of the value of some kind of provision for pre-school children, the country has continued to neglect the under-fives.

A survey carried out by the National Union of Teachers (*The State of Nursery Education*, 1964) showed that the average waiting list for nursery schools had 108 names, or one-and-three-quarter times the actual number of children who could be accommodated in the nursery. 'In other words, the total demand for places (including those who have obtained entry) exceeds the supply in a ratio of eleven to four.' In a third of the schools, parents were expected to wait for two years before having their children accepted.

Not only was there an acute shortage, but official government action, instead of stimulating the provision of nursery schools, actually trimmed it in 1960, when it issued Circular 8/60. This admitted that it had been impossible to implement the relevant sections of the 1944 Act. 'It has not at any time ... since the Act came into operation been possible to undertake any expansions in the provision of nursery education.' Nevertheless, 'no resources can at present be spared for the expansion of nursery education and in particular, no teachers can be spared who might otherwise work with children of compulsory school age.'

In the entire history of modern British education this is the only case of an actual official embargo being placed on the provision of nursery schooling. It would be wrong to place the entire burden of blame upon the Ministry of Education, which was faced with an unprecedented shortage of teachers and a growing volume of children coming into the primary schools. Indeed, given the whole previous history of neglect of the under-fives, the 1960 Circular was inevitable. It is, nevertheless, a major barrier which still exists. Two Addenda to the Circular, one in July 1964 and another in December 1965, have slightly eased the position, in that they have permitted the extension of nursery schooling where a local authority can guarantee that this will result in the release of mothers for teaching.

The position now is a little clearer:

Each of a local education authority's first three nursery classes must accommodate sufficient teachers' children to 'produce' an extra four teachers: an authority with more than three classes yielding at least twelve teachers is allowed to expand its nursery provision, so long as 'the number of qualified women teachers whose service in maintained schools is facilitated by their children's attendance at any of the authority's nursery schools remains at least twice the number of teachers who are employed in the authority's nursery schools and classes as a whole'. (Addendum No. 2 to Circular 8/60, December 1965.)

Despite the Addendum's expressed view that 'nursery education is primarily designed for the benefit of children, and is only secondarily of value in helping to promote the return to service of married women teachers,' the Department of Education has taken (or been forced to take, depending on how charitably one considers its role) the official position that the care of the pre-school child can be disregarded, and that nursery education, where it is provided, is fundamentally a tool for releasing women for other work. This is an extremely dangerous principle to have adopted and it has created the precedent of viewing the nursery school as a sort of *crèche* and a source of adult labour. The Department is thereby open to the accusation that it is officially encouraging mothers to abandon their children for an outside job, while discouraging the positive education of young children, a curious position for any Department of Education to take up, especially as it carries with it a built-in social bias. This suggests that nursery schools are suitable places for the children of middle-class parents who themselves have a good education and where mothers may be freed from their responsibilities to take up employment, but they must be closed to children whose mothers' educational backgrounds disqualify them from work demanding higher educational qualifications – that is the essence of the present position, regardless of the liberal sentiments that frame the Department's regulations.

The result of regressive policies of this kind is that since the Committee of Enquiry presented its liberal and forward-looking document in 1929 there has been scarcely any advance in the provision of nursery schooling in England.

Chapter Eight
The Statistics of Pre-School Provision

In 1932, about 5 per cent of the under-fives in the country attended either schools or nurseries, or their full-time equivalents. In January, 1967, the figure was about 8 per cent. But there are great difficulties in trying to find just how many children are receiving some form of pre-school education, care or welfare. History has bequeathed a tangled web of largely unrelated services and uncoordinated legislation for the young child, and where this has proved inadequate, private enterprise and charity have added further components. Central statistics are hard to come by, and even when they are available, remain open to a range of interpretations. Even with all the figures available, the calculations can be done in an almost infinite variety of ways.

Howe (1966, p. 24) described the confusion this way:

The Nursery Schools Association in *The Under-Fives in the Welfare State* concludes that only 3 per cent of children under five are receiving some kind of nursery care; but they exclude children at private nurseries and those with child minders and they calculate their percentage as a percentage of *all* those under five and not as a percentage of two to fives. The Fabians, in *New Patterns for Primary Education*, arrive at a figure of 6 per cent; but they exclude children at independent primary and all-age schools. The Department of Education concludes that 9·9 per cent of the two to fives are at schools of some kind; but this figure includes the 'rising fives' (who attain the age of five later in the term for which the figures are quoted) and excludes all those in Ministry of Health provision. The Nursery Schools Campaign Committee in their general policy statement have produced the most alarming figure of all. 'Nursery education', they state, 'is available to only one per cent of the two to five age group'. It is just possible to arrive at this figure if one ignores *everything* except maintained nursery schools.

Since then, the Plowden Committee has quoted a figure of 6·9 per cent for the total provision of children under five, but included the 'rising fives', all the provision made by both the Ministry of Health and the Home Office, and set the total against the child population between 0 and 4. The Seebohm Committee on Local Authority and Allied Personal Social Services, taking its cue from Plowden, has also talked of 6 per cent but did not produce its own statistics.

From these varying analyses, it can be readily seen that the statistics depend as much on who is presenting them as they do on the hard facts. In particular, it depends on which items are included and which are excluded; on which are regarded as educational in content, and which are more clearly classified as 'welfare'. A baby placed in a *crèche* for the day while its mother goes out to work cannot be thought of as receiving some form of pre-school education. On the other hand, it could be argued that any child that finds itself in some socializing environment – such as that provided by a registered child-minder, for example – is to that extent enjoying an experience that might go beyond 'welfare' and towards 'education'.

It is as well, therefore, to consider the varying forms of welfare and schooling available at present and to classify these as best one can, so that the differences are clear.

At the national level, there are the maintained nursery schools, many of them the legacy of provision provided before the Second World War or just after, which do not usually take children under the age of two, and often prefer not to have them until three. Places are free and attendance may be part-time or full-time. Nursery classes in primary schools are equally free and many places in direct grant nursery schools, where costs are partly met by government grants, are also free. Independent nursery schools charge between twelve and thirty guineas a term, regardless of whether the Inspectorate recognizes them as efficient.

Within this provision there falls a large group of children, described as the 'rising fives' who are approaching their fifth birthday, and are, where accommodation is available, accepted by their infant school somewhat earlier than the date when it is obligatory for the school to do so. The Department of Education and Science and the Plowden Committee both included this large group (some 134,000 in 1966) as falling within the 'pre-school' population; as a result, their calculations have given a rather rosier picture than is strictly warranted. For by pre-school provision one does not mean those who, on a purely local basis, may find themselves lucky enough to get taken in by their infant school a few weeks earlier than is legally necessary, but rather, planned provision for the two to fives, a category which may include, but only at the extreme end, those children who are nearly five years old.

Yudkin (1967, p. 32) made the same point, in commenting that the official statistics are not justified in including this category.

'The very high proportion of the actual places (almost half) which are occupied by the 'rising five' children make these figures quite misleading. Real nursery education is effectively available for a much smaller proportion of the under fives.'

Consequently, Table 2 considers only those children who can be said to enjoy a 'pre-school' education in the strict sense; they are being given experiences designed for those not expected to start formal schooling for at least another three months.

The next series of provisions to be considered fall under the control of the local authorities, and include *crèches*, where working mothers leave their babies or small children, day nurseries for the same purpose, nurseries run by factories for the benefit of their workers and private nurseries run for profit. Local authorities also register daily guardians who look after no more than two children under the age of five, and child minders, who have to satisfy the authority that they have the necessary premises and facilities to look after more than two children on their own. Under the Nurseries and Child Minders Regulations Act of 1948, pre-school playgroups can also be registered with local authorities in this way.

The third set of provisions fall to the responsibility of the Home Office, and include foster homes for children, homes provided by voluntary organizations or foster parents recognized by such organizations or a local authority.

To consider all these diverse provisions together is to mistake their widely differing aims and, indeed, the age for which they cater. In calculating the extent of the provision, therefore, I have taken different stated objectives to arrive at three separate statements.

The first is an over-all assessment, as near as statistics will allow, of all the provisions made for children under the age of five years, whether done privately, under the aegis of the Ministries of Health or Education or the Home Office, or of local authorities. That gives us an over-all figure, against which we can place the known total population of children under five.

This is not quite as useful a guide as it might seem, because the provision for children from birth to two years is different in kind from that for children from two to five, because it is inevitably incomplete and also because the quality and aims of the care involved are so very varied. There is, therefore, a second measure which we can take. That is to look only at the *educational* provision provided specifically for the under-fives. This rules out child minding, *crèches*, day nurseries and a number of other, largely welfare, organizations, but includes places at maintained nursery schools, all nursery classes, private nursery schools and classes and play groups. Here we can compare the provision against the known population of the two to fives, although again this is not strictly accurate, because many nursery schools and classes do not take children until the age of three.

Finally, there is a measure of the official provision for the education of the under-fives. Here, the variables involved are only the maintained and direct grant nursery schools, nursery classes and special and hospital schools. I have again excluded the 'rising fives', but taken as the measure the number of three to fives in the community. In each case, therefore, the yardsticks are rather different.

A further difficulty occurs with the statistical sources. For some categories, official statistics are non-existent. A case in point is the extent to which pre-school playgroups cater for the under-fives. Here I have relied on the estimates made by the

1968 survey of 1020 playgroups by the Pre-School Play-groups Association (see Keeley, 1968), but inevitably there is some overlap between these figures and those produced by local authorities for registered child minders.

Again, official statistics do not normally break down the ages of children under five in nursery schools or classes into those between two and four and those who are 'rising fives', but figures supplied to me by the Department of Education and Science do contain such a breakdown and I have used these to present a new figure for pre-school children in maintained primary schools – a figure considerably different from those normally quoted.

In some cases, the figures used by official enquiries, such as those for the Seebohm Committee, differ from those given by the Department of Education and Science, either through a difference of interpretation or possibly a difference of source. In some cases, the variations are considerable. Once again the playgroups situation provides a good example. In the P.P.A. survey, it is suggested that 88–9 per cent of some 3000 playgroups were registered with their local authorities. Yet the statistics provided by the L.E.A.s certainly does not reflect this large number of private pre-school groups, or the number of children involved.

The statistics used in Table 2 are drawn from a wide variety of sources. They come, primarily, from the official statistics of the government agencies: Education, Health and Social Security and the Home Office. But in addition, I have used a number of secondary sources, such as the 1967 Plowden Committee (*Children and their Primary Schools*), Dr Simon Yudkin's (1967) report, the 1968 *Seebohm Committee Report on Local Authority and Allied Personal Services*, and in one specific case, the 1968 P.P.A. survey of 1020 playgroups (Keeley, 1968).

Table 2
Total Provision for Children up to Five Years in
England and Wales, 1967

Type of establishment	Nos.	Full-time places	Part-time places
Grant-aided nursery schools	462	23,939	9044
Nursery classes in maintained primary schools	—	63,591	—
Direct-grant nursery schools	15	656	280
Recognized independent nursery schools	9	267	128
Other independent nursery schools[1]	162	3907	1776
Recognized independent schools other than nurseries[2]			
Primary		2497	
All age		1690	
Other independent schools other than nurseries[3]			
Primary		8128	
All age		2638	
Maintained special schools and hospital schools	91	1661	
L.E.A. day nurseries[4]	444	21,169	
Private nurseries run by factories[5]	56	2095	
Other private nurseries[6]	4382	109,141	
Daily guardians and L.E.A. registered child minders[7]	865	1482	
Pre-school playgroups[8]	3200	80,000 (est.)	
Registered child minders[9]	5039	42,696	
Local authority homes: boarded out[10]		15,029	
Homes provided by voluntary child care organizations[11]		3584	
Boarding out by voluntary organizations[12]		521	

If we tally all provision made in 1967 in this way, substitute one full-time place for every two part time places and measure this against the population aged from birth to five years in 1967, we get an over-all figure of 9·3 per cent for the total provision for the age group; in other words, less than one child in ten.

If we now take our second measure, that of educational provision, we leave out all specifically welfare organizations but include the pre-school playgroups and once again allow one full-time place for two part-time places. We now set this against the total two to four population for England and Wales in 1967, and arrive at a figure of 7·7 per cent; that is, 7·7 children in every hundred.

Finally, if we look only at the official provision for education for the under-fives and repeat the exercise, considering only maintained or grant-aided places in nursery schools and classes, and once again leave out of the reckoning the 'rising fives' and all independent provision – if we set this against the three- to four-year-old population of 1967, we arrive at a figure of 5·7 per cent or almost half the figure normally quoted by government officials.

1. The *Seebohm Report* quoted markedly lower figures for this category. It said that there were 118 institutions dealing with 1899 full-time pupils. Appendix F. para. 66, p. 261.

2. *Plowden Report (Children and their Primary Schools)*, vol 1, p. 109.

3. *Plowden Report*, op. cit.

4. *Seebohm Report*, Appendix F., para. 223, p. 288.

5. *Plowden Report*, op. cit.

6. *Seebohm Report*, op. cit.

7. *Plowden Report*, op. cit.

8. P.P.A. 1020 Playgroups Survey, p. 7 (Keeley, 1968).

9. *Seebohm Report*, op. cit.

10. Home Office, *Children in Care in England and Wales*, March 1967, part 1, table 1.

11. Home Office, op. cit.

12. *Plowden Report*, op. cit.

Chapter Nine
The Geography of Deprivation[1]

However statistics are juggled, the point is inescapable: we are not making enough provision for the under-five age group. That is the truism of recurring statistics. But that statement is only meaningful if for a moment we assume all under-fives as enjoying equality of opportunity and of social environment. Britain has a very imbalanced society; so it is more relevant when talking about the shortage of nursery provision to look at those who need it most, and then to consider what chances they have of obtaining such provision. This involves looking, therefore, at 'need' within society and somehow trying to match this against 'provision'. It is not an easy exercise because in this area of the under-fives most of the central information is either not collected in any form that makes it accessible, or is simply not available. This immediately becomes clear if one were to pose the question: how many educational priority areas (E.P.A.s) are there in the country and where are they sited? It is obviously a matter of a sensitive interpretation of local conditions, and not a question of data gathering. One has to be on the ground, as it were, to see such areas and to decide which are the priority areas for improvement. In many cases, it is the spin of a coin that will decide the issue. Sometimes the areas shout out aloud for themselves, they are so bad. But often they are matters of subjective interpretation.

But when the Plowden Committee did quantify need, it came down on a figure of 15 per cent of the age range which needed full-time nursery education, and it calculated this on rather different parameters to those it had laid down for the definition of E.P.A.s. It took into account such factors as the number of working mothers, numbers of mothers identified as unable to cope with their children and also poor environmental

1. This chapter is based on a paper given to The National Conference of the Nursery Schools Association, May 1968.

factors. The Gittins Report (*Primary Education in Wales*) which dealt with primary education in Wales, pointed out in strong terms the plight of children living in rural areas: their isolation, the liability for their growing up in aged, industrially declining communities. Here again is a factor that might define 'need'; but again, it is difficult to quantify.

Dr Jean Packman (1968) examined the reasons for applications for care and for committals to care in forty-two sample authorities during six months in 1962. In this study she discovered forty-five different reasons why families might find themselves in need. The reasons fell into six groups: incomplete families, health, poor home conditions, child difficulties, miscellaneous and court orders. Of these six categories, the most significant was the breakdown of the normal family unit, either through death, imprisonment, illegitimacy, divorce, desertion or separation. Ill-health, and particularly mental illness, was also a major factor, as was homelessness. Now it is arguable that a number of these factors may be more prevalent in E.P.A.s, but many of them are not, nor are they the prerogative of any single strata of society. What we therefore learn from the Plowden, Gittins and Packman reports is that, clearly, there do not appear to be isolated patches in England and Wales where need is notably greater than elsewhere. There are E.P.A.s everywhere and although the geography of deprivation may be mottled, in the sense of an impressionist painting, it covers the entire canvas.

This is reinforced by the evidence from the statistics of the National Society for the Prevention of Cruelty to Children, which draws its cases from every one of its 215 branches throughout the country. It is by looking at these statistics a little more closely that one gets an inkling into the 'intensity of the geography', if I can use that odd phrase. In the first place, while the number of cases dealt with by the N.S.P.C.C. has dropped (this is because of the provisions of the 1963 Children and Young Persons Act, which now insists upon local authorities carrying out preventive social work), the drop is less than expected; and in the totals for children of five and under, the decline – which one might think ought to be considerable – was no more than to bring the figures back to the

1956–7 level. This seems odd when the law, which before did not allow an authority to initiate help, now permits it to go out into the field and actively offer aid. It is curious that this did not result in a greater decline in N.S.P.C.C. cases. One of the reasons is that the Society's inspectors are locally well-known and trusted, and that people in trouble often prefer to go to them than to consult a local authority officially who may still be relatively new to the area. Even so, there must be many other factors at work, and the problem is important to this study, for today very nearly half of all the N.S.P.C.C. cases involve children of five or under; and the percentage is going up. This figure is borne out by the findings of Dr Packman, who gave the following distribution of children in families at risk (see Packman, 1968, p. 48).

Table 3
Distribution of Children in Families at Risk

Age of Children in Families at Risk

Age of children at home	All questionnaires %	Committals to care %	Long-term admissions %	Short-term admissions %
under 2 years	22	9	25	23
2–4 years	26	15	20	28
5–14 years	47	61	47	46
15–17 years	5	15	8	3

From the N.S.P.C.C. figures, we can get some idea of the trend. Since 1963, when the Children's Act was passed, the total number of cases handled by the Society has gone down from a peak of 121,500 to, in 1967, 93,000, and the total number of cases affecting fives and under has dropped from a peak of 54,200 to, in 1967, 44,000. But the statistics of the N.S.P.C.C. since 1963 are only part of a much larger picture. When we want to look at the trend in deprivation, we have to ignore the latest figures, which are distorted by the passing of the 1963 Act, and consider the graph of the statistics from say, 1957 to 1963. If we do this we find a steady climb: from 102,500 in 1957, to 104,500, then to 106,600, then on to 112,000 in 1960–61, to nearly 118,000 the following year and then another leap to 121,550 in 1962–3. What is even more disturbing about this rising tide of cases being dealt with by the N.S.P.C.C. is that, within these over-all figures, the proportion of those dealing with children aged five and under gets larger every year. In 1957–8, for example, 43·6 per cent of the cases involved fives and under, but by 1962–3 the percentage was 44·6 of a much larger total. In numerical terms, it looks like this: in 1957–8, 44,679 children of five and under were dealt with out of a total of 102,461 cases. In 1962–3, 54,273 children of five and under were treated from a total of 121,565 cases.

What all this means is that there appears to be a rising tide of need; it is not a static situation. Although it is not now possible to arrive at a total figure of children of five and under being handled by either the N.S.P.C.C. or the local authorities, it is certain to be considerably in excess of 35,000, or nearly 100 children a day identified as being in need of care or protection. Inspectors sometimes say that for every case they actually handle, there are another nine that they do not hear about. Taking a conservative figure of only half this amount, we come to the fact that in the population of some four million children between birth and five years there are perhaps 175,000 in immediate need of preventive treatment: some 4½ per cent. And if we then add the criteria laid down by the Plowden Committee, to include children of working mothers, of children living in poor environments, then the numbers seem to rise beyond the 15 per cent mentioned by Plowden and may go as high as 25 per cent of the total.

A recent survey by Audrey Hunt on women's employment found that 14 per cent of mothers with children from up to two years, and 20 per cent of mothers with children from three to four were working. Emphasized in that report is the extent to which children of working mothers are looked after by other members of the family. 'In many instances children were cared for, or expected to be cared for, by their grandmothers who themselves had worked little, if at all, since their marriages. It cannot be assumed,' concluded Miss Hunt, 'that when the present generation of children has grown up their mothers will be as willing to accept responsibility for their grandchildren.'

At present, only some 6 per cent of the infants of working mothers included in this survey are cared for in day nurseries, whereas 40 per cent are looked after by a relative and 25 per cent by their fathers. If, as one suspects, this pattern is likely to change, then here could be one of the reasons for the rising tide of child need.

But whatever the reasons – and it is fair to say that virtually no research has been done on this question – the present statistics still do not suggest the geographical pattern of that need. Until a few years ago, it was not even possible to contemplate even looking for such a thing. But the 1963 Children and Young Person's Act has provided at least one statistical advantage. For the first time it is possible to consider the number of cases handled by local authorities under both the Children's Act of 1948 and the 1963 Act. The 1948 Act empowered local authorities to provide for children referred to them by welfare authorities; the 1963 Act gave them additional powers to give advice, guidance and assistance. If the two sets of powers are taken together, we can arrive at a total figure for the demand made upon a local authority. This total demand has been called the 'bombardment' figure by Mrs Barbara Kahan, the Children's Officer for Oxfordshire County Council. To arrive at some idea of existing need, however, it is also necessary to take into account the provision that already exists within a local authority to meet this 'bombardment', and a very rough guide to this might be obtained by looking at the number of children 'in care' in a local authority. Where, therefore, we find an authority with a 'high bombardment' and a low 'in care' figure, it might be thought that there is a figure of 'need' that is not being met. This is an arbitrary test and not very satisfactory, but the best we have at present.

The second column in Table 4 deals with the percentage of this 'bombardment' figure received 'into care' during the twelve months up to 31 March 1967; indeed, all the statistics deal with the period 1 April 1966 to 31 March 1967, the most up-to-date figures available.

The average 'bombardment' figure for counties is 13·1; for

boroughs it is 22·6. The average 'in care' figure for counties is 4 per 1000 and for boroughs it is 6·4 per 1000. The interesting interpretation of these figures is to see those areas where bombardment is higher than average and the percentage in care is lower than average: notably Radnorshire, Cheshire, Rutland, Staffordshire, Brecknockshire, Lancashire, Nottinghamshire among the counties, and Cardiff, Halifax, Rochdale, Bury, Wolverhampton, Hull and Southport among the boroughs.

To indicate how arbitrary the provision of pre-school facilities is, four more columns have been added to the table. The fourth gives the total number of known full-time nursery school places provided by the relevant authority. The fifth and sixth gives the number of under-fives – not 'rising fives' – in either nursery classes or reception classes in primary schools in those areas. The last column is merely a total of columns four and five.

To be more helpful, the final column in this table ought to give an indication of the percentage of under-fives in the area being given some kind of educational provision. Unfortunately, our current statistics have not reached that degree of sophistication. Nevertheless, the figures do provide some rough measures. Hampshire, with a slightly higher than average 'bombardment' figure and a slightly lower than average 'in care' figure, has only fifty-eight pre-school places. Dewsbury, with a lower than average 'bombardment' figure and a higher than average 'in care' figure, has four times as many pre-school facilities; and so on.

It is true, of course, that the 'bombardment' figures as well as the 'in care' figures apply to all persons under eighteen, whereas the nursery school figures deal only with under-fives, so that these two sets are not directly comparable. What is notable, however, is that 45 per cent of children in care are, in fact, five years or under. Dr Packman's table (Table 3), above, makes the same point.

The real point of these figures is inescapable. There is no correlation between the apparent 'need' and the provision of nursery school places. Nor do the provision of pre-school playgroups or nursery classes started under the provisions of Addendum 1 and 2 of Circular 8/60 change this situation.

Table 4a
'Bombardment', 'In Care' and Educational Provision
Statistics for Under-Fives 1 April 1966 to 31 March 1967.
By county

1	2	3	4	5	6	7
County	Bombardment figure	% of col. 2 received into care	No. in care per 1000 under 18	Full-time nursery school places	Under-fives in maintained primary schools	Total of cols. 5 and 6
Caernarvonshire	41·7	25·7	4·7	41	1037	1078
Lincs (Holland)	26·5	13·0	5·1	—	42	42
Oxfordshire	25·2	10·9	9·4	36	327	363
Denbighshire	24·9	12·6	5·6	—	1081	1081
Herefordshire	22·6	16·0	6·2	33	59	92
Radnorshire	21·8	2·7	2·8	—	44	44
Cheshire	21·7	7·3	3·2	29	856	885
Somerset	19·6	14·0	3·9	71	209	280
Rutland	19·4	16·0	2·0	—	4	4
Glamorganshire	18·6	9·4	4·5	423	4707	5130
Northamptonshire	18·2	13·5	4·2	58	172	230
Dorset	18·1	20·0	5·7	—	135	135
Lincs (Lindsey)	18·0	15·0	5·0	52	70	122
Staffordshire	17·7	9·0	3·2	596	663	1259
Breckonshire	17·6	8·0	3·2	24	559	583
Lancashire	17·5	11·4	3·0	1321	4503	5824
Huntingdonshire	17·2	21·6	5·2	71	260	331
Nottinghamshire	15·5	13·0	3·1	81	149	230
West Suffolk	15·0	17·0	4·0	—	82	82
Lincs (Kesteven)	15·0	22·0	6·1	90	43	133
Hertfordshire	14·6	22·0	4·4	620	349	969
Northumberland	14·5	16·0	5·5	—	474	474
Isle of Wight	14·4	27·9	5·1	—	64	64
Hampshire	14·0	23·0	3·7	39	19	58
Monmouthshire	13·8	12·4	3·4	388	360	748
East Suffolk	13·7	25·0	6·6	—	71	71
Wiltshire	13·4	21·3	4·2	—	82	82
East Sussex	13·4	25·0	5·8	—	199	199
Worcestershire	12·9	13·0	4·2	39	132	171
Norfolk	12·6	9·6	2·8	118	366	484
North Riding	12·3	22·0	4·8	44	124	168
Derbyshire	11·3	20·9	3·4	71	870	941
Buckinghamshire	11·1	23·3	4·1	278	525	803
Warwickshire	10·9	28·0	4·3	330	345	675
Bedfordshire	10·4	23·0	4·2	154	97	251

1	2	3	4	5	6	7
County	Bombardment figure	% of col. 2 received into care	No. in care per 1000 under 18	Full-time nursery school places	Under-fives in maintained primary schools	Total of cols. 5 and 6
Pembrokeshire	9·9	15·0	2·6	—	215	215
Devonshire	9·9	22·8	2·8	—	67	67
Berkshire	9·8	20·0	5·4	361	93	454
Kent	9·6	24·0	4·9	36	327	363
Westmorland	9·5	24·0	2·9	53	126	179
Essex	9·4	23·0	3·2	33	290	323
Salop	9·2	24·0	4·5	105	129	234
Cambridgeshire	8·8	24·0	4·5	192	452	644
Cardiganshire	8·6	6·8	4·1	—	267	267
Anglesey	8·4	7·3	1·7	—	492	492
Merionethshire	8·3	22·9	4·2	—	278	278
West Sussex	7·8	34·0	4·3	91	88	179
Cumberland	7·7	36·0	4·0	40	67	107
West Riding	6·7	32·0	4·2	422	2734	3156
Gloucestershire	6·1	27·0	3·3	40	256	296
Flintshire	6·0	21·8	4·1	30	1098	1128
Surrey	5·7	41·0	3·7	43	94	137
Durham	5·5	28·0	3·3	806	648	1454
Cornwall	5·4	31·9	5·3	40	50	90
East Riding	5·4	37·0	2·6	40	138	178
Carmarthenshire	4·4	51·0	3·7	—	1411	1411
Montgomeryshire	2·0	47·0	2·4	—	167	167
Leicestershire	—	—	—	—	7	7

Table 4b
'Bombardment', 'In Care' and Educational Provision
Statistics for Under-Fives, 1 April 1966 to 31 March 1967.
By borough

1	2	3	4	5	6	7
County	Bombardment figure	% of col. 2 received into care	No. in care per 1000 under 18	Full-time nursery school places	Under-fives in maintained primary schools	Total of cols. 5 and 6
Tynemouth	79·3	6·8	8·4	5	70	75
Derby	69·6	8·9	8·8	115	372	387
Cardiff	68·5	4·4	5·7	402	185	587

1	2	3	4	5	6	7
County	Bombardment figure	% of col. 2 received into care	No. in care per 1000 under 18	Full-time nursery school places	Under-fives in maintained primary schools	Total of cols. 5 and 6
Oxford	58·0	10·2	11·0	280	233	513
Halifax	55·6	14·5	5·4	65	315	380
Burnley	47·9	16·0	5·8	406	304	710
Reading	43·4	7·9	5·6	184	140	324
Salford	39·1	17	7·4	178	302	480
Preston	38·3	19	6·9	98	171	269
Bolton	38·3	9·8	6·3	174	906	1080
Rochdale	37·7	13	5·4	303	70	373
Bury	37·2	7·5	4·5	39	64	103
Walsall	35·7	4·4	6·7	115	20	135
Wolverhampton	35·7	5·4	4·3	20	239	259
Oldham	33·7	30	8·2	120	556	676
Chester	31·0	13	8·3	80	150	230
Hull	30·8	15	4·2	—	—	—
Portsmouth	29·1	19	9·7	42	167	209
Grimsby	27·9	11·3	6·3	44	151	195
Nottingham	27·7	20	7·6	87	537	624
Leicester	27·7	27	8·6	19	1459	1478
Hastings	26·6	29	6·9	—	64	64
Bradford	25·8	22	8·5	183	506	689
Bournemouth	25·8	13	9·9	—	98	98
Norwich	24·5	16·6	7·8	90	344	434
Birmingham	24·2	21·4	7·0	1078	1458	2536
Plymouth	24·1	21·0	9·6	—	132	132
Southport	24·0	19·6	2·0	178	302	480
Manchester	23·0	30·6	8·9	204	3514	3718
Wallasey	22·7	44·7	4·4	16	—	16
Barrow	22·2	23·8	3·4	106	119	225
Warley	22·2	4·0	3·0	—	—	—
Lincoln	21·9	27·0	6·7	90	55	145
Swansea	21·5	8·7	3·7	230	536	766
Carlisle	20·7	11·5	4·5	—	8	8
Brighton	19·9	31·0	8·0	24	495	519
Exeter	19·5	25·0	4·9	23	24	47
Burton-on-Trent	19·5	12·0	4·5	—	46	46
Luton	18·2	13·8	3·8	133	51	184
Southampton	18·0	24·9	8·3	—	172	172
Bristol	18·0	19·0	9·3	857	466	1323
Leeds	18·0	23·0	7·0	28	248	276
Stoke-on-Trent	17·8	16·0	5·9	775	1075	1850

I	2	3	4	5	6	7
		% of	No. in		Under-fives	
	Bomb-	col. 2	care per	Full-time	in	
	ard-	received	1000	nursery	maintained	Total
	ment	into	under	school	primary	of cols.
County	figure	care	18	places	schools	5 and 6
Middlesbrough	17·7	17·7	5·2	—	225	225
Worcester	17·1	24·0	6·3	—	101	101
Gloucester	16·9	29·8	7·2	—	127	127
Merthyr Tydfil	16·8	2·9	4·0	30	78	108
Newcastle	16·6	5·0	8·7	85	214	299
Blackpool	16·0	27·0	5·4	—	8	8
Sheffield	16·0	32·0	6·7	254	903	1157
Bath	15·9	13·7	4·4	—	316	316
West Bromwich	15·6	9·0	4·3	—	119	119
Newport	15·2	25·0	6·1	142	201	343
Liverpool	15·1	44·0	5·3	359	779	1138
Southend	14·7	23·0	5·0	—	78	78
Warrington	14·5	48·9	8·7	—	449	449
Eastbourne	14·5	12·0	7·2	—	30	30
Coventry	13·8	26·0	5·2	57	484	541
Huddersfield	13·0	48·0	4·9	—	11	11
Rotherham	13·0	3·8	7·1	105	173	278
South Shields	13·0	28·0	5·5	—	38	38
York	12·8	11·3	5·9	39	150	189
Great Yarmouth	12·3	36·2	4·2	39	150	189
Bootle	11·5	41·0	2·9	—	118	118
Doncaster	11·4	20·4	3·3	—	384	384
Dudley	11·1	10·9	3·0	144	35	179
Stockport	11·0	29·0	7·2	264	66	330
Darlington	11·0	34·0	6·9	200	82	282
Gateshead	10·8	44·0	6·1	40	68	108
St. Helens	10·4	24·0	5·9	—	577	577
Ipswich	9·5	39·0	3·8	39	17	56
Barnsley	9·3	26·0	4·1	40	271	311
Canterbury	8·8	0	4·3	—	26	26
Northampton	8·0	15·0	6·3	87	537	624
Birkenhead	7·5	42·3	4·9	—	178	178
Sunderland	7·5	40·8	5·7	15	45	60
Blackburn	7·4	56·0	7·0	120	729	849
Wigan	7·4	20·2	5·8	—	433	433
West Hartlepool	7·0	6·7	5·8	84	4	88
Dewsbury	6·6	42·0	8·0	134	84	218
Wakefield	5·3	17·8	4·7	—	355	355
Solihull	4·4	33·8	1·5	—	56	56
Smethwick	—	—	—	80	277	357

Chapter Ten
Self-Help in Local Communities

Although the need for pre-school provision is national, it is local in its immediate effect. Many parents, conscious of the possible divisive effects of the fee-paying pre-school playgroup, have tried to wrestle with the current restrictions to provide at least some form of stable and organized pre-school educational experience and these kinds of experiments have recently taken a new turn.

Stevenage has, on a rough calculation, some 4000 children under five without a single nursery school in the vicinity. Moreover, being a community of young working people, the area was under great pressure some years ago to provide enough primary school places, so that even the chance of 'rising fives' being admitted into infant classes was remote. The homes provided for the New Town settlers normally contained only one large living room and a small kitchen, so that the children on the new estates were denied a whole range of experiences with water, clay, sand and other materials, and this lack created immense local pressure for some kind of pre-school provision.

The concerned parents of Stevenage began by forming a local committee which attracted a local Justice of the Peace, a health visitor, an expectant mother, a nursery nurse and the headmistress of the local infant school. From the outset, this committee turned its back on the normal kind of pre-school group and aimed instead at a nursery class established in proper premises and staffed by professional teachers. It was fortunate in being able to use the hall of the Bedwell Community Centre, where it seemed possible that a group of thirty children could be taken for week-day classes at a fee of twelve shillings and sixpence per week to meet the running costs. The group set out to achieve its objectives by launching a capital fund to provide equipment, registering itself with the local authority under the Nursery and Child Minders Act, calling in the Fire Protection Officer to cover possible problems of hazard and at the same time getting a grant from the Urban District Council towards the cost of equipment. The school opened on the 9th January 1958 'with a qualified teacher of young children, a nursery nurse, nine children and faith'.

In order to achieve this major objective the committee was involved in a considerable administrative programme. It had to open a bank account. It had to raise money by arranging raffles and obtain a licence to run such fund-raising ideas. It had to approach local industry for materials for the class. It had to deal with the landlord of the premises about the storage of these materials and about the use of the building. It had to liaise with the local health committee about the size of the accommodation, the toilet accommodation, the number of staff to be employed and the outdoor playing area. It had to make formal application to the Divisional Medical Officer for registration; to the owner of the premises for an agreed tenancy; to the Ministry of Health for free milk. It also had to deal with the problems of national insurance for the staff.

The tenacity to pursue such a programme is not given to all volunteers, and even when it is achieved, the nursery class set up by each voluntary effort still suffers from the divisiveness of a fee-paying institution. The committee running Bedwell, for example, wanted to reserve two places for non-fee-paying children in the early days of the class as a service to the community, but almost immediately a salary scale increase ruled out such a possibility.

But the experience gained by setting up this first voluntary class spread to other parts of Hertfordshire and was used to set up other classes. In particular, parents in Hertford followed the Bedwell model and set up a similar class in a guide hut staffed by a professional teacher and guided by a County Adviser in nursery education. After two years of running classes in this hut, at three shillings a day for each child, the whole project was threatened with closure to allow the building of a relief road. According to one of the organizers, 'the committee was adamant that the school should continue. When it consulted a local education official it was given a sympathetic hearing and sound practical advice. But there was no building in the town which could be used, no empty classrooms and it became clear that a new building was essential.' Then the Hertford parents took a look at their local primary school and suggested to the school managers that there appeared to be space on the site for the building of a special nursery class. The Council gave its consent to such a project and the County Architect's Department advised on its siting and construction.

What the nursery committee now had to face was the capital cost of constructing the class, but to their credit they had two years in which they had proved their ability to administer such a class and, as a result, they had the wholehearted support of their local authority. Indeed, this support took a very tangible form. Under the provisions of the Physical Training and Recreation Act of 1937 and 1958, which empowers L.E.A.s to make grants and loans to voluntary organizations for capital works provided these are for 'athletic, social or educational purposes', the Council made a 15 per cent grant, amounting to £570, towards the cost of the building. The Borough Council gave £500 and the students of the local college of education subscribed the total proceeds of their annual rag, another £500. The committee itself raised a further £300, and for the balance of some £1900 the County Council offered an interest-free loan repayable over twenty years.

The result of all this organization and fund raising was that a new prefabricated building meeting the most stringent official requirements was built by public subscription on the site of the local primary school for the specific use of pre-school children, and the parents needed to find only £95 a year to repay the loan, without being tied to a lengthy programme of fund raising with its inevitable delays. It meant, also, that the voluntary programme had advanced from providing, in the first place, playgroups in sometimes inadequate premises plus amateur tuition, to properly organized classes under professional guidance in an environment linked directly to the educational provision of older children.

Both these pioneering efforts demonstrate the extent to which local initiative can force the pace in the provision of nursery education, but they both also displayed the shortcomings of such efforts. Both ventures were dependent on the fees paid by parents for such facilities, reinforcing the weaknesses inherent in the pre-school playgroup provision. They remained enclaves of middle-class ambitions and inflexible in their ability to vary the intake into the classes or provide a more wide-ranging service for the community as a whole. On the other hand, they illustrated how nursery school provision, instigated with determined voluntary help, could be integrated into the educational facilities of the community.

It is to overcome some of these problems that a further venture is now being tried at Lewes on the South Coast. Lewes falls within the East Sussex Education Authority which only has one nursery class, at Newhaven, under its control, and that a relic from the post-war years when classes vacated by evacuated school-children were appropriated for the younger ones. Lewes itself has no nursery provision, although it has an estimated population of some 500 between the ages of two and four. Near-by Brighton, in a different L.E.A. area, only has two nursery schools, the vestigial remains of an ambitious plan after the war when forty-two sites were earmarked for nursery school development following the 1944 Act.

In the circumstances, Lewes has inevitably thrown up a variety of pre-school playgroups. But a number of local mothers realized that the circumstances of such groups severely restricted their ability to serve all sections of the community. Classes run in homes, or church halls, imposed a barrier of fees, imposed amateur tuition and cut the intake to those who could afford to send their children. How could these problems be overcome? The mothers came together to find a solution and to re-affirm their attention of establishing a nursery class attached to one of the local primary schools, with the object of drawing the attendance to such a class from as wide an area of need as possible. In this they were encouraged and supported by the headmistress of the largest local primary school. The next step was to explore ways to realize their goal and so they began to investigate the labyrinth of official policy towards such a scheme. In particular, they needed to know the conditions under which an L.E.A. might set up a nursery class, whether there was any way in which they might obtain official financial support for such a move and whether the Department of Education's minor works programme – for building projects under £2000 – might be harnessed to provide such facilities. The answers were not encouraging.

Although under Section 8 (2) (b) of the Education Act, 1944 local education authorities are required to have regard to the need for nursery schools and nursery classes in other schools, it has not so far been possible to allow any general expansion in nursery provision because all our resources have been concentrated on providing for children of compulsory school age, but more recently because of the shortage of teachers, particularly women teachers trained for work with young children. However, provided conditions set out in Addendum 2 to Circular 8/60 (see Appendix, p. 165) are complied with, local education authorities may now provide nursery facilities.

In order to set up a new nursery class, an authority which has fewer than three nursery classes in existence must be able to identify four qualified women teachers who would place their children in the proposed nursery class and teach in schools maintained by the L.E.A.s. Suitable accommodation must be available which can be adapted, if necessary, at a minimum cost. Any minor buildings work involved will fail to be met from the Authority's current minor works allocation.

This advice restates the classic official position. In the case of Lewes, where a local authority was anxious to help but could not provide the necessary resources, the Secretary of State for Education provided even greater clarification, which add a number of riders. In a letter to an enquiring M.P. he said recently:

Although a local education authority may not establish a new nursery class under the terms of Addenda 1 and 2 to Circular 8/60 unless it can show that there will be a net gain in the teaching force, it does not follow that where that condition can be fulfilled, the authority is obliged to take action. They may already, like East Sussex, have all the teachers they need or (a particularly important point at the present time) they may be unable to make adequate financial provision for additional educational facilities not required for children of compulsory school age.

This latter difficulty is not met by the provision from voluntary resources of the necessary building, since the most expensive element in nursery provision is the cost of maintaining it and running it. There is no way of making additional money available from Government sources by way of special grants or loans and local education authorities have no power to give direct financial assistance to voluntary associations or groups which make this type of provision for themselves.

This discouraging interpretation of the present conditions does not entirely fit the facts. The Bedwell and Hertford examples have shown that where a local authority is enthusiastic about nursery education, it is prepared to make substantial financial assistance, on terms which are only marginally commercial in character, to assist voluntary workers. Nor is the accounting problem quite as simple as the Ministry has made out. If, for example, a new nursery class can provide educational facilities for handicapped or referral cases from the welfare authorities, this might actually cut the burden on these local divisions, in which case there might be a transfer of funds from the one to the other. Similarly, although the burden of maintaining a nursery class is undoubtedly the major item of expense for any education authority, the Lewes case showed that this cost, involving twenty-five children in the morning and another twenty-five in the afternoon, was no more than about £3000 a year.

What became obvious in the Lewes case was that much depends on the interpretation of the local authority of the rulings under Circular 8/60 and its Addenda issued by the Department of Education. Lewes was fortunate. It found considerable sympathy in its local authority, and as a result, the approach by the voluntary committee with a proposal to provide a building from private funds was accepted by the L.E.A. on condition that guarantees were given that the statutory number of qualified teachers would be released as a result of the venture. In addition, the building itself had to be approved by the County Architect, the school managers had to be in agreement and the estimates had to be prepared about the running costs. The building, as in the case of Hertford, had to meet the necessary requirements of providing at least twenty-five square feet per child, and meet health regulations about sanitation, lighting and heating. Finally, all the details had to be submitted to the Department of Education and Science.

But what was most important – and that which makes Lewes's experiment unique among voluntary efforts to provide nursery education – was the agreement that was reached between the mothers and the local authority about the nature of the intake. All along, the aim had been to overcome the problem imposed by fees which cut out many working-class children, and by unsuitable accommodation which shut out handicapped children. In the evolving scheme at Lewes, it was now decided that the selection of pupils for the nursery class would be decided by giving priority to the following groups:

(a) The children of the married women teachers who would be enabled to return to teaching.
(b) Handicapped children from the whole of the Lewes area, providing that the number of these children did not exceed 25 per cent of any one class.
(c) Children from outside the normal school area, for whom there was a social need for nursery education, provided again that their numbers did not exceed 25 per cent of any one class.
(d) Children from the area itself, about the half the size of any class, priority again being given to those in social need.

This remarkable agreement marks a considerable advance on any previous experiment for meeting distinct social needs in nursery provision in a locality. It does away with the fee-paying barrier while providing at one and the same time a professionally conducted education environment, built into the existing school framework with the specific aim of taking in a comprehensive range of children, some of whom might come from areas not immediately served by the school. In this sense the nursery class is interrupted, rightly, in my view, as not merely educational experience for young children but in some way as a remedial unit where children from different sub-cultures and different developmental stages and even with different physical handicaps can come together and learn from each other. What remains important in such a class is the role of the parent, and this is an area where innovation and experiment will point the way. The great value and lesson of the pre-school playgroup movement has been the involvement of mothers in the education of their, and other people's children, and any move towards a more integrated pattern of nursery class development, such as at Lewes, ought not to lose sight of such a virtue. It remains, therefore, to evolve a scheme of activities within the voluntary sponsored nursery class which will actively involve the mothers and which will enable them to feel an essential part of the operation. One immediate advantage of the Lewes pattern is that in taking handicapped children, for example, there will certainly be a need for mothers to provide extra hands to cope with their particular problems. Lewes does not yet have its nursery class. When it materializes, there will be an opportunity to set many more precedents. In the meantime, it has shown how, given the understanding and co-operation of local government, apparently insurmountable obstacles can be overcome creatively.

What characterizes the Hertford and Lewes case studies is the involvement of parents and local people in education. But until that education can be made more effective, until the instruments of social diagnosis can be sharpened we are still dealing, in the case of the under-fives, with pretty crude tools. On the one hand we have local attempts to provide the children with facilities which can already be provided, given only that the money and will are there. On the other hand, two attempts are now under way to improve the state of the art itself. The Plowden Report's major contribution to educational thought was to translate into an English context the idea born with Operation Headstart in the U.S. That is to say, it stressed the inequality of our social system in terms of educational opportunities fostered by that crucial variable, the home environment. For the first time, a positive discriminant was introduced by a post-war education committee to provide special help for what was called the educational priority areas;

areas so rundown in physical and economic terms that the environment is likely to prove a positive handicap to the education of young children growing up in them. The Plowden recommendations about help for the E.P.A.s have not been fully implemented, but a start has been made. Some 400 nursery classes, providing full-time places for about 10,000 children, at a cost of £2·7 million were approved by the Department of Education and Science early in 1969. The programme also included provision for some new day nurseries and children's homes, for teachers' centres, in-service training courses for teachers, language classes for immigrants, transport facilities, educational equipment, family advice centres and aid to be given by local authorities to voluntary bodies to provide playgroups, centres, adventure playgrounds and advisers. Within the programme there exists the possibility of more nursery schooling for L.E.A.s are entitled to give this high priority and to gain additional funds for it. But the overall figure for expenditure over the next four years is limited to between £20–25 million.

The question that has since arisen is how money of this kind can be best used. Is it better, for instance, to stress the support system for the young children, or to concentrate on help for the mothers? Given limited resources, should these be aimed firmly at the educational sector, or in welfare services, or in a combination of both? And if a combination, what kind of combination is most fruitful? This is the kind of question that local teams, under the general direction of Professor J. A. Halsey, are investigating with the help of the Nuffield Foundation. It is also the subject that has attracted the attention of the Schools Council, in its *Project in Compensatory Education*. Taking its cue from the Plowden recommendation for E.P.A.s, this project is concerned with studying the factors within the social fabric that cause some children to 'lose out' in their schooling, 'those children who would otherwise drift downwards through the classes of the education system, ending up in the remedial groups, the special classes, or the bottom end of the lower streams in junior and secondary schools.'

The project will not only study the social background of

groups of children and the progress those children make in their first three years in school, but develop materials for the teaching of some of these children, as well as collecting a great deal of data on the social and educational variables within the communities and their effect upon educational performance.

Studies such as this, in the field, hold the promise that in the future the discussion of nursery provision will become a good deal more socially adaptable than they are at present and that the role of the nursery class or school will eventually change from the largely post-Froebel philosophy in which it still finds itself, to one much more designed to cope with the infinite variety of problems that affect young children.

Chapter Eleven
The Day of the Nursery School

'When you catch a rainbow, can you actually touch it?'
'Please, how quick is time?'
'What makes the chimney pots move sideways past the clouds?'

The questions that young children ask reflect the inner turmoil of their minds as they try to reconcile the structure of their new-found language with the empiric evidence of their senses. A nursery school is full of such questions. Its aim is not merely to encourage them, not even just to provide sympathetic answers, but to produce an environment in which young children can both be stimulated into questioning and can find, in their surroundings, answers from their own experience. Once again, this is an over-simplification, because children who are disturbed in one way or another – and few children exist who are not troubled by some incidents in their life – need a therapeutic environment in which the wounds of experience are healed sufficiently for them to turn away from their introspection and enquire about the world about them. This theraphy is an incredibly complex process, little understood but instinctively practised by the good nursery school teacher.

In a little nursery school in one of London's most affluent areas this kind of therapy is an unspoken but daily routine. About thirty children attend the school for the full day, and another dozen come only for the morning. Two large rooms are filled with all the bric-a-brac of child play – puzzles, Wendy houses, rocking horses, bricks, books, trains, wooden toys, cooking materials, paper and crayons, scissors and paste, water, sand and every conceivable activity to muse and instruct the small child. Tables and chairs of child dimensions are scattered informally throughout the rooms and the children are totally free to move from activity to activity, coming together in different groups. A third small room is kept as a 'secret hide-away', a store room that is normally closed to adults and in which children may seek a refuge from the teachers and helpers in the school. In this small room three girls may build themselves a house out of wooden blocks and chairs, and organize an elaborate household. Two boys might work out a secret trap for one of their friends, or a single child, wishing to be alone and undisturbed, may find a haven here.

But it is the garden that is their real delight. To the un-initiated visitor it might at first seem a dangerous place for children, with masonry and uneven paths forming hills and rockeries and flower beds; with a sunken garden, a sandpit, and a clutter of play equipment, including a complex of scaffolding and step ladders that provides an endless source of exercise and inventive play. There are nets for climbing, and an extended net for swinging and bouncing. There are work benches for woodwork and special areas for digging. An out-side tap can provide water for puddles or a hose. Planks of wood are available to be turned into pirate ships, tanks or homes. All is ready for instant conversion into the fantasies or realities of the child's mind.

It is an unstructured day that children spend in such a school. Once they have put their coats away and settled down, they are free to turn to anything they wish. This freedom is often a release for those who come from homes which, how-ever 'good' they may be in the socio-economic sense, still act as a restraint on the demands of a rapidly developing child. The initial response will be violent bursts of energy, wild aggression, an uncoordinated exuberance. Sometimes the violence has other origins. Repressive parents, or parents who squabble constantly in front of a child, or a death in the family, all leave their marks on a growing mind. They create an aura of instability, an environment which is unsafe or in which the small child feels insecure and unloved.

It is easy to find the children who face such particular difficulties. If a visitor confines himself to observing the activities of the children and makes no move to communicate with them, they will accept his presence but ignore his personality and carry on with their interests. But if the visitor shows an interest in them, seats himself among them, questions their activities and comments on their performances, he is immediately flooded with a band of children who seek to hold his hand, to cling to him, to sit on his knee, to monopolize his attention, to adopt him as a substitute parent. He is regaled with anecdotes, with unending recollections of past incidents, with stories about their families, with elaborate descriptions of their ventures. These are not children being simply friendly and out-going; their natures demand a thirst for an attention that has not been satisfied in the past. It might take the form of violence, with a child hitting the visitor repeatedly, clinging to his legs, hurling punches at him. One child, who had just knocked two pieces of wood together to make an aeroplane, saw its potential as an axe and lashed out with it at me:

'Do you want to hurt me?'

'I am going to smash you up.'

'Go on, then, knock my fingers off.'

He lashed out, and hit my fingers. I bent the fingers into the palm of my hand.

'Now see if you can knock my hand off.'

He hit out again, catching my hand. I bent my hand at the wrist, and pretended he had knocked it off.

'Are you going to knock my arm off?' I asked, bending it at the elbow. He hesitated, wondering how far he could go. Then he burst out laughing. I laughed too. He put down the rudimentary axe and ran off to play. He had recently lost his father.

One is reminded of a note Susan Isaacs once kept of a child who attended the Malting House School (see Chapter Thirteen). The boy

shows more hatred in his expression than any child I have observed. His opening remarks when coming to the school were: 'I will kill you! I will shoot you! I will hit you in the face! I will kill you blind dead! I will throw you on the roof so that you can't get down!'

This violence needs careful handling. It needs understanding and it needs organization. It must not be repressed, but at the same time, it cannot be allowed to vent itself on other small children. Parents find it incomprehensible that nursery teachers should allow what to them is such violent anti-social behaviour, just as they find it impossible to understand that A. S. Neill, the pioneering headmaster of Summerhill School, Leiston, Suffolk, once went around his school with a disturbed child and the two together threw rocks at the windows until most of them were broken.

Most of the released violence at a nursery school is not so drastic and consists of little more than rushing around, and the occasional fight or knocking down of bricks. The very presence of other children, and the social code that their presence imposes, acts as a restraint. The important feature is that in the environment of a good nursery school repressions have an outlet and that once released the child can be free to divert his attentions away from his own immediate problems and direct them at the world at large.

In a permissive atmosphere such children blossom. At this particular nursery there were some very bright children. One small girl was a balletomane and although she could not yet read she had surrounded herself, at the age of three, with every book on ballet she could find in the school. She recounted in detail the entire story of *The Sleeping Beauty* ballet she had recently seen, and added the scenario of *Puss in Boots* and *Treasure Island* for good measure. More than that, she could open one of the books and point to a particular dancer, giving his name and recalling that she had seen him dance a particular role.

Next to her, another small child recalled, with infinite detail, the range of cars and their makes that her uncle had possessed. Names like Lancia, Cortina and Renault came easily to this child, who had an almost photographic mental record of the specifications of each vehicle.

The development of these children occurs in concert. Even though they may not become close friends, their very presence in the same house creates a social climate that is beneficial to all of them. The school abounds in social opportunities for children to come to terms with others. They can wander into the kitchens and help themselves to milk or simply go and talk to cook. Their teachers and assistants are constantly available for advice, succour or stimulus. Their mothers are free to wander in and stay with the children or come and fetch them home. Visitors are constantly strolling in, either to gain their first impression of nursery life or, as students, to watch more closely the behaviour of young children. At the end of the morning and afternoon sessions, after the bustle and noisiness of free activity, a sudden hush falls on the school as the children quietly gather their chairs together and listen communally to a story.

It is an intense world of incredible activity, raw on the ears of those who believe that children ought to be seen and not heard, but welcome to an increasing number of parents. The Plowden Committee found that not only did 73 per cent of primary school teachers believe that all children whose parents wanted it should be exposed to such experiences, but the Committee's National Survey enquiry into parental attitudes (*Children and their Primary Schools*, vol. 2, appendix 3, tables 41 and 42) showed that a third of the parents would have preferred their children to have started some kind of schooling before the age of five.

Pregnant mothers are known to sidle past the doors of another London nursery school and try to engage the head mistress in a spirited conversation that inevitably ends with a query as to whether their unborn child could be put down for attendance. The school, in the heart of the hotel trade and flanking some of the seamier East End areas, refuses. With a population of ever-moving families around it, it wisely waits until children are at least two years old before putting them on the waiting list and does not accept them into the school before the age of three.

The nursery is 'purpose-built' – it was designed as a nursery when the building went up in 1930. Consequently, it has the kind of child-centred architecture that all good schools should have, with wash basins of the right height, a washroom and cloakroom to every playroom, simple access from the playrooms to the play area outside and large windows that allow plenty of light. It could still be better: there are heavy swing doors in the corridor that challenge the strongest five-year-old. They keep out draughts and children at one and the same time. There is not enough light in these corridors, and the paint could be gayer. But despite this and the heavy-jowled, squat exterior of the thirties, the building also has many virtues.

Basically there are three large rooms all equipped in much the same way. In this space some fifty-three children spend most of their day, arriving at quarter past nine in the morning and leaving at quarter to four in the afternoon. In addition a further thirty-three children come just for the morning period, going home at 11.45 a.m. and another thirty-three come just for the afternoon, arriving at 1.20 p.m. At the last count this school had a waiting list of 140 names and was receiving applications at the rate of twenty a month.

All sorts of children come to this nursery school. Many of them live in high blocks of flats. Many others are the victims of the hotel trade. One child was kept sitting in a high chair in the same room in which the central heating plant operated. He arrived at school grossly overweight, scarcely able to move his limbs. Other children are the offspring of university staff and might reflect either good environments or be the subject of that particularly cold and impersonal neglect that charac-terizes better educated parents preoccupied with their careers. Many of the children come from overseas, or have parents who are not themselves British, and consequently have difficulty with the language. None of them have to pay to attend this subsidized nursery school, but most make a voluntary contribution of some kind and many parents join a special parents club to take a personal interest in the affairs of the school.

It is a place that inspires interest. From the brass rubbings hanging on the walls of the entrance hall, to the gay patterns of children's paintings that crowd every space in the play-rooms themselves, this is a world dominated by the child, his creations, his discoveries and his needs. There is an abundance of potential experience packed into every corner. A rabbit munches lettuce in the hall. Racks of books stand in every room. Easels, pots of paint, each with its separate brush, and sheets of paper clipped to the boards with clothes-pegs, wait ready for the creation of the artist. Sand trays, woodwork benches, clay, collections of shells, Wendy houses packed with toy dolls, cots, tea sets and model furniture, toy cars and garages, counting material, pegboards and puzzles, baskets full of fancy dress materials, and masses of paper, pencils, crayons and plasticine wait neatly upon low shelves for the childhood impulse to reach out.

Outside, sandpits and rope ladders, tunnels, hoops and slides, rocking horses and cars stand ready to be clambered upon, swung aloft or shaped into castles or moats.

A trained nursery teacher is in charge of each of these three rooms and a trained assistant helps her look after the children. In addition nursery students and a number of other helpers move about constantly in attendance. But there is no coercion and little actual guidance. Apart from the morning and after-noon drink of milk, the sessions around the piano, the compul-sory rest period on camp beds and the morning and afternoon story sessions in the reading corners created next to each room, the adults maintain the discreet role of advisers and friends. 'If we told them what to do, it wouldn't be them doing it, would it?' was the simple, direct philosophy expounded by one assistant. There is a spirit of mutual co-operation and respect between adult and child that is striking to the visitor. One child, slashing away at a piece of paper with a brush loaded with violent colour, announced that the painting was finished. With infinite care, the assistant removed the com-pleted sheet from the board and hung it to dry over a clothes-hanger. It was not crumpled up, or thrown away, or called a mess. It was accepted as a piece of work, an individual act, and treated in exactly the same way as the painting by another girl, done with infinite care and the gritting of small teeth, that turned into a gay and fetching clown.

A stranger who walks into such a school is struck by the mature way in which the children move, by their apparent lack of concern at the approach of visitors.

'That looks very gay, Susan,' I commented on one little girl's work with coloured scraps of paper.

'How do you know my name?' she asked, without looking up.

'It is written down on the top of this sheet.'

'Yes, it is,' she replied. 'And that is Mary and that is Caroline. What is your name?'

This mature approach is also reflected in their social behaviour towards one another. In one room a small girl was curled up asleep in a doll's chair. She had been like that for some time, but the half-dozen other children in the room with her took no notice. There was no attempt to wake her, to shout, or, on the other hand, to muffle the natural noise of their play. She was left to her own devices, with an unconscious respect for her privacy and her personal desires.

The children are governed by few rules, but show a natural respect for those that do exist. While they may occasionally baulk at tidying up materials after they have used them, this takes the form of a diplomatic haggling with the assistants as to how much help they are going to get with the task. All accept readily that they need to wear aprons while painting, and when they occasionally forget to take them off and dash out into the garden to play, they immediately remove them on being reminded.

It is a gay, busy, intense world, to which the children are introduced gradually, with their mothers coming in frequently. After a short while – no more than a week – the child is immersed in it, restricting himself at first to the familiar activities, but gradually learning from the others what other possibilities exist and extending his interests until finally he has mastered an enormous range of experiences the variety of which is astounding.

In the hallway two boys with upturned boxes are involved in a mysterious, inexplicable game. A third sits on a large wooden truck which he pushes with his legs. Three girls are holding an involved tea party in a Wendy house. Two boys are pushing pegs into numbers, the number of pegs relating to the value of the number. 'Thirty-eight, thirty-nine, forty ...' murmurs one boy under his breath. In one corner a boy all alone reaches into two big wicker baskets and pulls out blocks of wood which he carefully arranges into a long railway line. Utterly absorbed, he brings an engine from a shelf and begins to push it along the line. Two girls sit, like old ladies at a bridge party, chatting, while their fingers knead clay into small cakes that are gently placed in a cake mould. Three other girls spread their hands out on sheets of paper and draw the outline of their fingers. Then they fill the tracing with a multitude of coloured pieces of paper.

A small, squat and intensely dark African boy rummages among the games on a shelf, and brings forth a mathematical puzzle. Singing a song under his breath he begins to fit various coloured blocks on to a set of pegs. On a wall, otherwise covered by paintings, there is a notice:

THINGS WE COLLECT: Matchboxes, old magazines, cotton reels, lace or ribbon, string, pieces of balsa wood, assorted boxes, old Christmas cards, unwanted story books.

As a nursery school this one has obvious points to recommend it, but it begs the question whether nursery schools themselves, as separate entities removed from the mainstream of educational thought and work, are desirable. As we have seen, their recommendation sprang originally from the poor quality of work in existing elementary schools which failed to cater for the needs of young children. Nowhere in Britain has education been so thoroughly changed as in the methods of teaching in the primary schools. The Plowden Committee Report paid handsome credit to this advance, which is evident to any visitor at any infant school. Many of the ideas that began with Froebel or Montessori have been adopted by the infant schools, so that they now bear no resemblance to those earlier classes. This being the case, is there still a need to segregate the under-fives from their elders?

Some would argue that there is, but in at least one experimental school in London the reverse is proving the case. At the Eveline Lowe School in Camberwell, children from three-and-a-half to nine come to their new school each morning and move into the same building. The youngest children have their own nursery, but the remainder are split up into family groups with age ranges from four to six and seven to nine. The entire school is one unit separated only by doors that can be opened by the smallest child. Although the costing of this new school was strictly controlled, it has certain obvious design advantages over the standard primary school. The equipment is lavish and of a high quality. There is an abundance of toys, wash basins, toilets for each class, quiet story-telling corners for each group, curtains and carpeting, that gives the school an atmosphere more akin to a modern home than an institution.

The children are drawn from the local neighbourhood and many of them have homes in high flats. For them the school is an oasis of child-centred activity in a harsh world of brick and mortar alien to their needs.

One teachers said:

When they first come to us, they seem overawed by the un-expected freedom they enjoy. They will come up to you and in a hushed voice ask: 'Can I use *all* this paper?' or 'Am I allowed to play with this truck?' or 'May I do that, too?' It is as if they cannot grasp the proportions of their freedom. But this soon passes. Sometimes it is only an hour or two before they have found their feet and then they give vent to a sudden burst of exhilaration and hyperactivity that can be deafening.

What is noticeable about the school, however, is the extra-ordinary social integration that takes place in it. Without any prompting a group of children, led by a potential Sarah Bernhardt, made up a play, used wooden blocks to mark out a stage and acted the whole thing out for their own amusement. It was obviously a vehicle for the leader's considerable histri-onic talents, but the others enjoyed it as much and there was no attempt to involve the teacher or impress anyone but themselves. A small boy who had hurt himself outside was being tended with great care by one of the girls. Three girls were having a quiet gossip in a carpeted area intended to act as a sitting-room. They poured each other cups of water and were obviously absorbed in their role as young housewives. A group of boys had used wooden blocks to build themselves a bus, and with a loose steering wheel were pretending to drive their friends through the neighbourhood. Two boys and a girl were at the work table, making 'magic pots'. One boy, very much a lone wolf, wandered around with a small screw-driver in his hand. Wherever a screw could be found, this child set to work to undo it. A special box of materials – front-door bells, bits of machines, an old gramophone – was his special delight. Faced with such opportunities for revealing the hidden secrets of technology, he was happy. And then there were the painters, using either their fingers or brushes, endlessly producing works to be hung up and dried.

Every now and then, these small children wander through to the rooms where their older brothers or sisters or friends are also at work. They share the hall for musical movement and an occasional assembly, but far more important, they are able to gain incentives from the older children and to take an interest in their work. They are not treated as a race apart.

The nursery section of the Eveline Lowe School has a practically unstructured day. Trays of milk bottles are left in the corridor for the children to help themselves. Every morning and every afternoon there is a special story session when the part-time children leave. Beyond this, the day is of their own making.

Unlike the nursery school, however, a much more conscious attempt is made to provide direct intellectual stimulus. At any time, children can demand the attention of the teacher and be directed towards certain goals. A boy who was weighing various materials on a scale was asked: 'Do you think one thing can weigh as much as a lot of things?'

'Let's see. If we put this big stone on this side, and we put a lot of these beads on this side, let's see what happens. Put some more on. What is happening? Now put some more on . . .'

Another group, playing about on a sofa in a special corner reserved for quiet reading and study, demanded a story. They themselves drew the curtains, switched on the light, screened off the area from the rest of the playroom by drawing a curtain across the opening and invited the teacher in. She complied and they got their story. Indeed, books abound throughout the school and any child at any time and any age can find himself with something to read.

No formal reading scheme is adopted by the school. As a child shows an interest in writing or has his name written on a painting or piece of work, he is encouraged to copy it or any other words that are of particular interest. From writing comes reading. Some of the four-year-olds, in addition, insist on being 'given a book' to read, following the example of their older brothers and sisters. Here the academic example of older children is particularly strong and beneficial. By aspiring to emulate their elders, the youngsters demonstrate a maturity and sophistication that is unusual for such an age group.

There is, of course, nothing new in the Eveline Lowe School arrangement. Welsh village schools often took children from two to seven, and the old, all-age schools similarly mixed their intake. The experimental London school was at least partly inspired by the Plowden Committee, which took great interest in its planning.

Unfortunately the Committee's investigations and the opening of the school did not quite coincide, so that the ultimate Report contains little mention of the project. Had the Committee been able to see the school in action, it might well have reconsidered its views about a national provision of separate nursery schools, needing their own sites and a duplication of many facilities that, in an integrated school, can so economically be shared. It is one thing to ask that local authorities set up a separate chain of nursery schools. It is quite another to authorize that new infant schools be so designed and built to cater for children from three-and-a-half years of age.

This change would also have other benefits. It would bring to an end the unhealthy segregation of young children from those only a few years, or even months, older. It would bring the – at present – pre-school child firmly within the ambit of the Department of Education of Science and allow infant teaching a wider range. It would do away entirely with the unnecessary anguish that at present accompanies the starting of formal schooling. By introducing small children on a voluntary basis, into the schools from three-and-a-half or even three, and by allowing them either morning or afternoon sessions, with full-time sessions only for those children whose mothers were out to work or whose home environment demanded it, school would cease to be a dread or a novel experience, and would become, instead, an accepted and normal feature of every child's early years.

Finally, it would place the emphasis where it belongs – on the educational needs of these children, rather than, historically and unfortunately, on the kind of 'social rescue' basis on which so many nursery schools still operate.

Chapter Twelve
The Evidence of Research

Anyone who has been associated with the education of young children or who has moved in the environment of a good nursery school, tends to be convinced, emotionally and intellectually, that the experience of such an environment is wholly beneficial to the child. So powerful is this feeling that few have taken the trouble to try and measure the extent of this beneficial effect or tried to isolate those factors appearing in later life which could be directly attributable to nursery schooling. The difficulties of doing this are admittedly very great and not immediately apparent. Even research workers in this field have been misled into thinking that these factors are easily measurable. Such a soberly academic figure as Dr Susan Isaacs, virtually the founder of child-development studies in England, was over-optimistic on this score.

In her book *Childhood and After*, written in 1948, she included a chapter on 'The educational value of the nursery school' in which she claimed that

by comparing children from the same sort of family and the same sort of general surroundings, of the same racial origin and the same degree of natural intelligence, we can measure more or less accurately the degree and direction of difference which the nursery school will make to their development. So far, all such studies have shown that children in the nursery school learn more easily, play more actively and thrive better in every way than similar children who have not this advantage, even if they live in good homes.

It is quite true that studies in America (Hattwick, 1936; Jersild and Fite, 1939; Mallay, 1935; Walsh, 1931) all seemed to indicate that children coming from nursery schools had an initial advantage over those children coming into infant schools straight from their own homes. Walsh (1931), for example, having paired a group of nursery children with another group having the same age, I.Q., general physical development and home background, found that her sample of nursery-school children were less inhibited, more spontaneous and more social at the end of six months in an infant class, than those children who had not been to a nursery school. They were, apparently, also more independent, showed greater initiative, were more inclined to assert themselves within a group, were more self-reliant, showed greater curiosity and demonstrated, on the whole, a greater maturity than their home-based friends.

Moreover, Hattwick (1936), having matched two groups of children and compared them after one group had been in the infant school six weeks and the other nine months, claimed that the impetus which nursery schooling gave children was measurably over and above maturation influences. Moreover he stated that those who experienced nursery schooling for some time showed distinct improvement in, for example, their attitude towards strangers, their play with other children and their general independence of adults.

Researches of this kind, however, have not been very convincing, not only because the samples of children have inevitably been very small, but because it has been so difficult to identify in the natural development of any one child the particular effects of either its nursery-school environment or its home upbringing. It has been found, moreover, as one might expect, that although nursery-school children, when first going into an infant school, have a head start over their less fortunate friends coming straight from home, these apparent differences do not last, and that after a year or two the other children tend to catch up.

A typical example of the kind of difficulties faced by any research worker trying to make measurements in this field are shown in a report by Deirdre O'Sullivan (1957–8). Miss O'Sullivan began with a series of highly interesting and relevant queries. Are children from nursery schools, where they have to learn to share, more sociable in the infant classes than their non-nursery contemporaries? Are they more friendly to strange adults? Do they have a wider vocabulary? Can they listen more attentively to stories and commands? Are they more energetic? Are their movements more controlled, more poised? Are they more ingenious in their approach to problems and in their use of materials?

To try to answer questions such as these she carefully paired eighteen children who had attended nursery schools with another eighteen who had come to infant school straight from home, matching them for home background, I.Q. and physical development. But after a great deal of work, which seemed to indicate that the children from nursery schools were slightly more forward in their vocabulary and their ability to listen receptively, she discovered practically no difference between the two groups in any of the tests she gave them. Some 470 pages later in her report, she was forced to the conclusion that

the results of this study, and of the many others on this topic, lead one to believe that there is little difference between children who have been in a nursery and those who have not. Yet the very fact that so many people have tried to find out if there is an advantage for the nursery children shows how strong is the feeling that there must be an advantage. To any one who has worked in a nursery, it seems obvious that this is so. But all those who have tried to prove it, have found very nearly the same results.

This leads one to question whether the qualities that one thinks might be improved in nursery children are measurable. Are there other ways in which these children are superior to others?

The only way to test the real value of nursery education would be to test each child against himself. This is impossible. Yet I can think of several children, in my own experience, who seem to have benefited from being in a nursery: one boy, in particular, who did not speak one word for six months. When he did start to talk, it was like a tap that would not turn off. He is doing quite well in the infant school now. Would he have been better by the time he was five, even had he not been to a nursery? Personally, I think not, but it cannot be proved.

Research dilemmas of this kind led a psychologist, Willard C. Olson (1957), to comment that both parents and professional people at times have hoped or assumed that attendance at nursery school or kindergarten would somehow be influential either in altering a child's general ability, or in assisting him to achieve greater success in subsequent years of school. The evidence is fairly clear that there are no special intellectual or growth effects attributable to attendance at a nursery school or kindergarten for children who have adequate nurture in their homes.

That seems a pessimistic appraisal, but at the time it was made it did appear that whatever the advantages were, they were impossible to measure. Inevitably, research workers concentrated on measuring the apparent differences between children in the first term of the infant school, although in fact there is no reason to believe that the effects of a nursery-school environment are most obvious at this stage. Indeed, one of the interesting side issues that emerged from one of these studies was the fact that, during the months of January and February, all the school children, whether they had been to nursery school or not, suffered some form of regression in their measurable development (O'Sullivan, 1957–8). It may be the case that the particular age of the children on whom studies were made coincided with a psychological phase of retrenchment, so that the differences were not obvious or at least not capable of isolation by research techniques. Equally, it might be that the effects of nursery schooling became more apparent later in school life and it would be interesting to look, for example, at the progress of children in junior schools to see whether nursery-school children show any apparent advantage.

But there are certain rather obvious social differences between children who have attended nursery schools and those who have remained at home that are apparent and can be measured. In the study made by Miss O'Sullivan, for example, infant-class teachers were emphatic that the effects were visible.

'You don't need me to point out the nursery children, they stand out – they always do,' said one teacher.

'They always come and ask if they cannot do something; they don't just stand and do nothing,' said another.

'They are more independent than the others; they can dress themselves and change their own shoes,' was another comment.

Other teachers agreed about their initial advantage but were more doubtful about the permanence of this advantage.

'They are more self-assured in the first few days. They have been used to a school routine and seem ready to enjoy new things,' said another teacher.

'They have the advantage of the others at first, but it doesn't take long for the others to catch up. After their first few weeks, you cannot tell the difference,' two other teachers remarked.

That the advantages really do go beyond a purely temporary head start in social attitudes was shown clearly by an extensive study carried out at the Child Development Centre at the Institute of Education, London University in 1959–60. Miss Marion V. Harrold and Miss Marjorie H. Temple considered forty-two children from four different infant schools, in an attempt, through observation, questionnaires and specific tests to assess the development of adjustment in those five-year-olds who had been to nursery school with those who had been admitted to reception classes straight from home. The questions they set out to investigate included the following:

1. Do children from nursery schools settle more quickly into the infant schools?
2. Are they more socially advanced?
3. Are they less frightened when they meet strange adults?
4. Do they make better use of language in their everyday association with children and teachers?
5. Is the quality of their speech better?
6. Do they display more vitality in their play?
7. Are there any differences between the two groups in physical confidence and agility?
8. Do the nursery school children show a better manipulative control?
9. Are they more ingenious in their use of materials in play?
10. Are they more creative in their painting?
11. Do they show more imagination in their play?

12. Are they more responsive to music?
13. Are they better able to take care of themselves, more independent?
14. Are they better able to sit and listen to stories?

All these factors are certainly ones which the enthusiastic supporter of nursery schooling would claim for their children but actually to measure the extent to which the claims are justified is a very difficult task. The research workers took twenty-one pairs of children and matched them for intelligence, age and home background. They were then tested in a number of ingenious ways. For example, a set of small toys was provided for the children to play with and during their play they were asked to talk about what they were doing so that an impression could be gained of their vocabulary and their use of language. In another test they were given objects like pins, paper-clips, beads, buttons and silver paper and asked to make anything they liked with the materials. They painted pictures during their class activities and these were later studied. They were asked to draw figures and the researchers then considered to what extent these drawings revealed their mental development. They were also observed constantly in their classroom environment and interviews and questionnaires were given to their teachers to analyse as closely as possible the behaviour of each child.

Some of the tests failed to produce any measurable results and some of the other questions, such as the response to music, were later dropped because it was not possible, in the circumstances of a busy school day, to carry out proper analysis. But enough emerged to show that there were real differences between the two groups of children. It was found, for example, that children coming from nursery schools were better both at the beginning of term and at the end of it in adjusting to the new circumstances of the infant school. They showed less overt signs of distress at the start of term and were also happier in the school environment. The nursery-school children were measurably better in their attitude to other children, in their self-confidence and in their response to the environment. They were more confident towards adult strangers in each case and they appeared to have a slightly better vocabulary. They had a slight edge in their physical confidence and agility and initially proved to be more ingenious in their use of materials. Finally, it was clear that the nursery-school children were more capable of looking after themselves and were generally more independent.

The research workers summed up:

In this particular group of forty-two children, those who had previously attended nursery schools were better in every respect except painting and manipulative control. They showed, however, a relatively greater degree of dependence on the adult for approval and recognition of what they had done. Certain of the children also showed an inability to settle to any chosen occupation, even at the end of term, and we think that this may be due to a lack of intellectually stimulating material in the nursery schools, which can lead the intelligent child to develop restless and unstable habits. The tendency of some of the nursery-school children to leave their toys where they had played with them instead of tidying them away may be due to the practice in some nursery schools of placing the toys on tables for the children's use. . . .

During the term improvement was shown by all the children, and the 'direct admission' ones made the greatest strides. Yet at the end of term the gap had not been closed, only lessened. . . . (Harrold and Temple, 1959–60.)

These comments indicate yet another pitfall for the would-be researcher looking for the beneficial effects of early schooling. Precisely because nursery schools are, on the whole regarded with favour, those children who have been to them are considered to have a basic advantage over those who have not. Obviously, however, nursery schools vary widely in the degree of stimulus and training they provide, and equally obviously there are great variations in the home environment even of children who, collectively, could be said to come from 'good' homes. The 'matching' of children from nursery schools with the 'control group' going to infant school straight from home is therefore crucial in any exercise of this kind; equally the analysis of the nursery schools themselves is a critical factor. In order to do any research at all it is often necessary to take quite liberal margins of variation in these matters and inevitably these will tend to make the findings less dramatic.

Nevertheless, the results that emerged from the Harrold and Temple survey were strong and they were made even more emphatic when they were correlated (in those cases where correlation was possible) with the findings of the earlier O'Sullivan research. In the case of the children's relationships and attitudes to strange adults, for example, the joint surveys produced the following marks:

	Direct admission	Nursery schools
Miss O'Sullivan's total marks	64	64
Harrold and Temple – attitude to teacher on first day	65	91
Harrold and Temple – attitude to observer during tests	46	80
Total	175	235
Number of children involved	59	59
Average score	2·96	3·98

(For full details of the criteria used by the research workers to obtain these marks the reader should consult the individual reports, the full titles of which are contained in the list of references on pp. 171 ff.)

It can be seen that in this particular aspect, the children who began in nursery schools have a distinct advantage. The position becomes far less clear when one considers a relatively vague aspect such as the degree of ingenuity displayed by the children:

	Direct admission	Nursery schools
O'Sullivan tests	45	46
Harrold and Temple tests	58	71
Total	103	117
Number of children	38	38
Average scores	2·71	3·07

Although the nursery-school children once again appear to do better than their colleagues, this is not a significant result, and no conclusions can be drawn from it. Tests for creativity or ingenuity are notoriously difficult to administer without bias and, in the case of very young children, it is almost equally difficult to assess the results, even assuming that all the children are fully co-operative. What was rather more simple to correlate were the two sets of questionnaires which the research workers gave to the teachers about the general development of their charges:

	Direct admission	Nursery schools
O'Sullivan questionnaire scores	865	931
Harrold and Temple scores	1193	1350
Total	2058	2281
Number of children	38	38
Average scores	54·15	60·02

Here again, the nursery-school children do slightly, but significantly, better than those coming to infant schools straight from home. It is notable in all such studies that, although very often the scores themselves do not give highly significant differences between the two groups, the nursery-school children individually appear to do better almost every time.

This is notable, too, in the detailed questions included in the two questionnaires presented to teachers by the research workers. Correlated, they give this kind of comparison between the two groups:

1. How do you rate the children for muscular development?

Direct admission		Nursery schools
3	very good	2
14	fairly good	21
16	adequate	11
3	clumsy	2
1	very clumsy	0

The nursery-school children seem, clearly, to be rather better developed muscularly than the others.

2. How is the manipulative control of the children?

Direct admission		Nursery schools
2	very skilful	1
5	skilful	11
22	average	24
8	poor	2
1	extremely weak	0

Again, the nursery-school children appear to have more among them who are well developed in this respect. As these children were carefully matched for physical development and age, the argument, at least on the physical side, for an early start in some form of schooling that permits plenty of manipulation of small toys, pencils, threading and so on, gains ground.

3. What is their attitude to parents?

Direct admission		Nursery schools
17	affectionate	19
9	casual	13
10	dependent	3
0	tearful	2
1	strained	1

Although the nursery-school children appear, on the whole, to be slightly more mature towards their parents, this is an inconclusive result. It gives an indication, if that is needed, that while children might be matched for observable, measurable factors such as age, stature and socio-economic background, there can be no matching of psychological disturbance and even a so-called 'good' home can create stresses and antipathies in the young child. I am inclined to the view that those with the greatest proportion of 'problem' children are not the working-classes, but professors of education!

When the research workers compared the self-confidence of these children, it produced this result:

Direct admission		Nursery schools
3	very self-confident	3
8	confident	17
18	average	14
8	little confidence	4
1	no confidence	0

Not a very significant measure, but nevertheless an indication that nursery-school children are, to a degree, more poised than their opposites. When we take the degree of aggression shown by these children, however, the picture is quite different:

Direct admission		Nursery schools
0	over aggressive	0
1	aggressive	2
12	average	26
22	mild	9
3	timid	1

'Nursery-school children are a frightful nuisance. They are so boisterous, always dashing here and there, forever getting in the way,' one head teacher commented to the researchers. These figures show what she means. The children direct from homes are much quieter and more subdued and, no doubt, a great deal less trouble to adults as a result. One can seen the same kind of difference when analysing their response to the school environment:

Direct admission		Nursery schools
2	investigates, explores	5
9	asks questions	17
17	observes quietly	13
7	shows little awareness	4
3	not at all interested	0

Now comparisons of this kind, while they seem to point to a clear initial advantage for the nursery school child in its first months in the infant school, also suggest that these children are more active, mentally and physically, more alert and one might therefore expect that they are more receptive to learning, to stimuli, than children who had not had this early advantage. Because measurable intelligence is so closely bound up with language and with the ability to manipulate abstract symbols, whether musical, mathematical or linguistic, it would be reasonable to suppose that this initial stimulus would, eventually, result in an over-all advantage to children with nursery-school experience.

As we have seen, it is very difficult indeed to provide factual evidence of this phenomenon. We know from the studies made by Dr J. W. B. Douglas (1964) that the formal education system as it at present exists in this country is self-fulfilling. By that I mean that examinations like the now-dying eleven-plus select children who then, because of a better and more intensive education, proceed to perform better than their less-fortunate colleagues. The prejudices in the system are self-reinforcing, so that, at the end, those who were selected at an early age can statistically be shown to have done better, partly because more was expected of them, partly because of smaller classes, partly because of the sigma of 'failure' that has clung around the secondary modern schools.

In such a situation, the residual effects of nursery schooling are obliterated by other, more recent, factors. The most recent attempt to measure the effect of nursery school attendances (Douglas and Ross, 1964) shows that even at eight, nursery-school children appear to do better than others. What the research also suggests, however, is that by the age of eleven this advantage has been lost and that by fifteen the nursery-school children are doing slightly less well.

None of these measures is statistically significant, but it might well be that the children selected for nursery-school education are in fact, those who, for one reason or another, are deprived in their home environment. These children may have received an intellectual boost from their nursery schooling. The question that inevitably must be asked is: how well would these children have done if they had not gone to nursery schools?

It remains true that the kind of children who, in England today, attend nursery classes are either drawn from homes where some kind of deprivation exists, or come from the higher socio-economic groups where nursery schooling is recognized as a valuable experience, to be supported and paid for. In either case, research on the subsequent progress of these children will be distorted by such factors. It must, in addition, consider the quality of the nursery teaching that they receive, as well as the standards of the infant, junior and secondary schools through which they move.

There is a further point. Nursery schools themselves still often see their role as being primarily social. The belief that pre-school children should, or ought, to be directly involved in intellectual stimuli is still not widely accepted. It is therefore of value to look at three experiments which set out, with almost missionary zeal, to provide such an environment for the very young.

Chapter Thirteen
In Search of Intellectual Development

The point has already been made that nursery-school education is considered a rare enough experience for comparisons to be made between children who have received it and those who have not, without questioning the quality of the nursery schools themselves.

Obviously, however, this quality is critical, and it is striking, in the examples that we have looked at, that the standard practice of even those good schools has not really advanced since the writings of Froebel and Montessori. So much energy has been expended in trying to provide nursery education at all that few have had the time or the money to experiment with new techniques.

From time to time, however, people who have been convinced of the thesis this book presents – that the intellectual development of the pre-school child is greater than most people suppose, and is being largely squandered – have set up particular pre-school groups with the aim of providing the kind of super-abundant environment that might dramatically contribute to the young child's intellectual development.

The most striking of these men in Britain was Geoffrey Pyke. On his death in 1949, *The Times* described Pyke as 'one of the most original if unrecognized figures of the present century.' After going to Wellington College and, for a short time, Cambridge, he became a war correspondent and made a spectacular escape from Germany during the First World War. Then he tried journalism, but eventually turned to the Stock Exchange, where a unique system of buying and selling metal shares brought him a small fortune.

It was with this money that, in 1924, Geoffrey Pyke decided to start a school for his only son, David, then three years old. Like Pastor Witte before him, Pyke contemplated spending his entire time educating his son. But because of the demands of the Stock Exchange this was impossible. Instead, he founded a school whose teaching would be based on scientific enquiry and where children would not be force-fed dogmas that pleased their elders, but where logic would be paramount and personal experiment and observation the keys to learning.

He once told a friend:

The fundamental principle we should follow in dealing with children is to treat every child as a distinguished foreign visitor who knows little or nothing of our language or customs. If we invited a distinguished stranger to tea and he spilled his cup on the best tablecloth or consumed more than his share of cake, we should not upbraid him and send him out of the room. We should hasten to reassure him that all was well. One rude remark from the host would drive the visitor from the room, never to be seen again. But we address children constantly in the rudest fashion and yet expect them to behave as models of politeness. If the principle suggested is to prove effective, there must be no exceptions. One rude remark to the child would give the game away. (Lampe, 1959, p. 211.)

To run his school, Geoffrey Pyke found a director in Susan Isaacs, then a young psychologist. The document they both helped to draw up at its founding read:

The general purpose of the Malting House Garden School is to provide, under expert and sympathetic supervision, the fullest opportunities for healthy growth in every direction, so that each child shall be free to gain control over his own body and knowledge of the physical world, to develop his natural interests, individual powers and means of expression, while living in a happy children's community, the conditions of which will lead to normal social development.

The school will, in the first instance, be designed for children of two-and-a-half or three years to seven years of age. (Van der Eyken and Turner, 1969.)

The children who came to this unusual school when it opened in Cambridge in 1924 were a remarkably bright group. Tests made a few years later, when there were seventeen children at the school, revealed that the average I.Q. of the pupils was 131, with a range between 106 and 140. At the same time, some of the children were deeply disturbed, and their presence placed a strain upon the school at a time when it was seeking to establish novel teaching techniques. 'It was sometimes said by outsiders, not by us, that the ten most difficult children in Cambridge had been sent to us,' wrote Susan Isaacs when the school opened. 'This was an exaggeration, but there were six or seven who were justly to be described as extremely difficult and one of these was on the border line of pathology.'

The other common factor about the children was that many of them had particularly intelligent parents, their fathers holding academic posts at the university. The school did not try to measure the extent of the increase in the I.Q. of its pupils as they progressed, but this would in any case have been difficult to assess, for many of the children followed a pattern schooling which reflected their own parents' particular view of education. They left the Malting House School to go to the Perse School, Cambridge, and then Bedales or Dartington Hall, followed by either Cambridge or Oxford University. But of those who stayed for more than a few terms, four were later to become academic members of staff of universities, one a medical consultant, one a teacher, another an actor, one a child psychologist and another a broadcaster. Of the girls, one married a judge, another an economist, a third a doctor. Nearly all the pupils did well, but this reflects as much upon their home environment, their innate ability and their subsequent schooling as upon any specific effects derived from the Malting House experience.

Susan Isaacs, in an unpublished article about the school, described its aims and methods in this way:

The key to the school is the growth of the children, and its methods must be based on direct observation of the children themselves. One of the most far-reaching changes of thought in human history is the modern view of the freedom of children as the basis of education. This is the great experiment of our age. Merely to give a vague and general freedom is, however, not enough. We must also observe what children do under free conditions, and study the laws of growth, so as to be able to meet their needs in detail.

In the Malting House School we not only give our children as much freedom of opportunity and choice as possible, but make a careful and exact study of their responses under these conditions, keeping detailed records, and adapting our methods accordingly.

The children are free to explore and experiment with the physical world, the way things are made, the fashion in which they break or burn, the properties of water and gas and electric light, the rain, sunshine, the mud and the frost. They are free to create either by fantasy in imaginative play or by real handling of clay and wood and bricks. The teacher is there to meet this free enquiry and activity by his skill in bringing together the material and the situations which may give children the means of answering their own questions about the world. . . .

The school provided an endless variety of experiences for the children. There were all the materials with which nursery schools are now familiar – coloured paper, plasticine, clay, shells, counters, beads, toys, Wendy houses, blackboard and chalks, paints, scissors and sewing materials. There was music and musical movement, and the garden contained a sandpit, trees, a canoe, a hammock, hen houses and things like watering cans for play. Later, each child had his own little plot of land and was given a set of bulbs to plant and tend. There were animals to look after, and a room full of wood and lathes for woodwork. There were also special toys, such as the see-saw with hooks along the bottom for hanging weights, which could be used as a measuring device. The children were taken on expeditions and were encouraged to dissect dead animals. Once they cut up Susan Isaac's old cat, which died at the school and on another occasion one of the children wrote to London Zoo to ask if any dead animals might be sent to the school.

But Geoffrey Pyke's own greatest interest was in providing a science laboratory for the young children. In this room bunsen burners, vices, glass test-tubes and a host of different materials were provided for the free play of the children. A master was put in charge of the room, to help but not to guide the children. One pupil many years later recalled to me the most vivid memory she had of the Malting House. 'I remember, in particular, helping to pour molten metal into a cold bath and watching it turn into different shapes.'

In a considerable evaluation of this school some years after it first opened, Susan Isaacs considered its effect upon the children in this way:

During the first and critical year the group life of the children went through a succession of well-marked phases. The first was one of brief quiet and subduement, due in part to the strangeness of a new place and new people; and in part, at least as regards the difficult children, to the expectation of the same kind of prohibition and punishment that they were used to at home. Then they began to wake up to the fact that over a large area of their desires and impulses the customary checks and penalties were removed. They found that they were free to shout and run, to occupy themselves in any way they liked, either with real material or phantasy and that at the first hint of quarrelsomeness they were not forcibly separated and spanked or scolded. Then followed an outburst of disorder and boisterousness, in which the aggressiveness of ten or eleven physically healthy boys of two and a half to five years of age found full vent. Throughout this period a considerable amount of constructive play went on, and there were many periods of happy co-operation and contentment, of friendliness and affection to the grown-ups.

But there were hours when the majority of the children were concerned merely in asserting themselves over against the others, sometimes in direct aggression, provoked or unprovoked, sometimes in destroying the activities of others and in open hostility to the adults present. Then, gradually, and with occasional resurgences of mere wild disorder, the group began to take a definite social shape, and the behaviour of particular children changed in the most remarkable way, until by the end of the year any typical day was occupied by constant free activity, with full give and take of friendly adaptation. The children showed an outstanding zest and pleasure in all their activities and a remarkable degree of free inventiveness, combined with a concrete appreciation of social realities. The change in some of the children was remarkable – the change from fear and peevishness and active hostility to calm and friendliness and freedom in play and cumulative activity. In some cases it was quite a dramatic change, leading to a sharp contrast between the school periods and the holiday periods. For example, the children of different families who had suffered from insomnia and night terrors from very earliest babyhood began to sleep regularly the whole night through soon after they came to school, continuing to do so during the whole term, and losing this within a day or two of the beginning of the holiday.

The statement of these remarkable changes in the social behaviour of the children does not rest upon any vague general impressions of my own, nor even upon the comments of the various visitors who came to watch the school at different times, but upon the records of the detailed observations of the children's sayings and doings which have been kept very fully throughout the whole period.

(These records formed the basis of two famous books by Susan Isaacs, *Intellectual Growth in Young Children*, 1931, and *Social Development in Young Children*, 1933. I have since been able to collate the entire record kept at the Malting House from 1924–9 and this is now the subject of further research.)

One of the extraordinary facts about the Malting House experiment is that although it proved to be a milestone in the emergence of child development studies, it was never financed from any source other than Geoffrey Pyke's private funds and when these came to an end in 1929 they were never supplemented from any official source. Nor, since that time, has any further experiment along Malting House lines been set up.

More recently a team at Teachers College, Columbia University, also considered the question of the intellectual development of the pre-school child. In this case the researchers (Wann, Dorn and Liddle, 1962) did not set up a school of their own, but studied three-, four- and five-year-olds in five schools in their neighbourhood. Three of the schools were day-care centres, one was a parent co-operative in a suburban community and the fifth was a private, church-sponsored school in a community of upper-middle and upper-class families. The total number of children studied by the team was 319, and these were observed, tested and questioned while they were active in their groups, with the object of finding out how much children understood about their world, what they wanted to know and how conditions could best be improved to stimulate their intellectual growth.

This study was launched to test the growing belief that children could know more at this early period than many educators believed possible. The belief grew from observations which pointed to the great range of interest and knowledge of young children and to the apparent satisfactions they derived from gaining and possessing information. The relative lack of concern in nursery schools and kindergartens for extending and clarifying their understandings and information was a source of concern for the researchers. (Wann, Dorn and Liddle, 1962, p. 2.)

For a period of about three months, the teachers in the schools made anecdotal records about their children and in particular of incidents or conversations in which a child seemed to be using a concept and applying it to his work or play. Forms for recording observations were developed to help teachers record the children's behaviour and words more accurately. Three test situations, using pictures, iron filings moved about on top of a box by magnets, and questions about family life, were used with small groups of the children. Finally, a number of specific experiences were planned and introduced into the school by the teachers. Most of these involved certain materials, such as a book on dinosaurs, a set of pictures showing the development of the aeroplane or a kit of materials demonstrating the properties of light.

The children's responses and their own unprompted conversations and actions were tabulated and analysed. The results, as expected, showed the enormous range of a child's world.

The children we observed demonstrated a great range of knowledge. The significance of our findings in this respect resides in the extent and depth of children's information and understanding and the great satisfaction they experienced in having information and being able to use it – it was clear that the interests of these young children were global, even universal in scope. (Wann, Dorn and Liddle, 1962, p. 18.)

The research team was confident that the environment of young children could be very much enriched to their benefit.

We have confidence in the insights we have gained about enriching their educational programs because we have introduced materials and experiences and then checked the results in a research way. We have indicated that we felt children today needed to have their intellectual abilities challenged and extended but there were few guidelines we could find to help us know how far to go in this direction. We were wary of overpowering children and none of us wished to over-emphasize this aspect recognizing, as we did, the importance of a balance among intellectual, social, emotional and physical development in young children. (Wann, Dorn and Liddle, 1962, p. 19.)

While the Teachers College study is a valuable exercise in the theory of pre-school education, it has the basic weakness of remaining a theory. A quite different approach to the intellectual development of young children is at present being tried by members of the Institute for Research on Exceptional Children at the University of Illinois. In their concern to help the under-privileged children of a predominantly Negro district of Urbana, in Illinois, they have begun a pre-school group which, quite determinedly, sets out to fulfil these children's educational requirements.

Fifteen four-year-old children, selected from poor homes in which the environment is particularly deprived, come to the school, which is run for two hours a day, five days a week.

When the children first arrived, they had, as expected, a minute repertoire of labels to attach to the objects they used or saw every day. All buildings were called 'houses', most people were called 'you'. Although Urbana is in the midst of a rural area, not one child could identify any farm animals. As obvious as their lack of vocabulary was their primitive notion of the structure of language. Their communications were by gesture (we later discovered that one boy could answer some questions by shaking his head, but that he did not realize that a positive shake of the head meant 'yes'), by single words or by a series of badly connected words or phrases.

The pronunciation of several of the children was so substandard that, when they did talk, the teachers had no notion of what they were saying . . . without exaggerating, we may say that these four-year-olds could make no statements of any kind. They could not ask questions. Their ability to answer questions was hampered by the lack of such fundamental requirements as knowing enough to look at the book in order to answer the questions: 'Is the book on the table?'

And again:

Only two of them came to the school with any knowledge of counting. None could repeat a simple arithmetic statement, such as $2 + 3 = 5$. None could read symbols. Only two or three knew that the answer to the question 'How many?' is a single number. Only about a third of them knew the concepts *same* and *different*. (Bereiter, Siegfried, Osborn and Redford, 1966.)

In order to give these children – all of whom were more than a year behind their better-off contemporaries in mental development – a chance to improve their mental skills before they entered the formal school system, it was decided to reject the approach of the typical nursery school and to concentrate, in a rather formal, no-nonsense way, on three vital aspects – the development of language, of arithmetic concepts and of reading. This was justified by the fact that these children not merely lacked any kind of mental discipline, but did not possess even the rudimentary equipment on which discipline might be based. Time for these children was short. What they needed was a kind of instant enrichment.

Because in this case the natural conversation of the children themselves was so limited the experimenters concentrated on establishing grammatical structure and sound pronunciation, so that the children could use the words they learnt in a variety of ways. 'Pattern drill' was introduced. To convey the idea of *big* and *little*, for example, the teacher might say:

'This block is big.'
Child: 'This block is big.'
The teacher might then ask: 'Show me the block that is big.'
The child might touch the big block.
The teacher might then reinforce this: 'Tell me about the block.'
Child: 'The block is big.'

Lessons of this kind, emphasizing the use of complete sentences and introducing simple concepts in a linguistic way, were carried out in small groups of four or five children. There were three twenty-minute periods, interspersed by one half-hour period for refreshments and singing, and a shorter period of relatively unstructured play activity. Each group had its own teacher and the groups were loosely streamed according to over-all ability and progress.

The experimenters also introduced the teaching of arithmetic as a language. Some of it was rote learning: 'One plus zero equals one, two plus zero equals two.' Problems were presented as questions: 'What's another way of saying $2 + 0? 0 + 2?$' Symbols were introduced in place of question marks to introduce the language of algebra. '$3 + 2 = a.$' The children were first taught to read the problem as if they were reading a passage of prose from a book, then to translate it into a question, and then to try to answer it. If the child could not actually tackle the problem straight away, he was encouraged to work it out by some analogous means. 'Let's take three fingers first. Now what does the statement ask us to do? It asks us to take two more. So let's add two more fingers. Now, how many fingers have we got altogether? So what can we write down instead of "a"?'

Using only lower-case characters and three-letter, consonant-vowel-consonant words, the children were also started on reading, and were even introduced to the basic structure of words and the rules governing grammar. Although these methods differ greatly from those that are normally applied in nursery schools and are in many cases opposed to the kind of teaching advocated for middle-class children, the question that really matters here is how effective they are in this particular case.

According to the research workers, three months of tuition along these lines has produced considerable progress. When the children first came to the centre, they showed, on average, a whole year's retardation when compared to their neighbourhood companions, and not one single child was performing as well in any of the subjects as his chronological age would allow. Approximately three weeks later, most of the children had improved by nine months on their earlier performance. By the end of the first three months, they had gained another three or four months in their performance, and were now, in some respects, doing as well as their chronological age would suggest. In those three months they had, in many ways, ceased to be deprived children.

In terms of the traditional achievement quotients, these children gained approximately twenty points in three months in three highly significant language areas. On two of them they are now close to normal. . . . Judged by absolute standards, it will be found that most of these children are still a long way from mastery of language, reading and arithmetic. On the other hand, their progress in three months' time seems to compare rather favourably with that of culturally deprived children in the first grade (six-year-olds) and these children are two years younger. In this sense the children are academically precocious, and in their general attitude and approach to learning this is how they act. There is every indication that the children will be able to maintain their present rate of academic progress. (Bereiter *et al.*, 1966, pp. 110–11.)

What we see, considering the three studies in the education of young children we have looked at here, is how little we know about the kind of enriching environment we ought to provide for them. It is almost certain that for any child special attention of the kind described here will elicit a strong response. The deprived youngsters in Urbana might well have improved their academic performance under almost any kind of programme, simply in response to an attention which, throughout their previous years, they had lacked. This is well-known to research workers as the Hawthorne Effect, which is a kind of shorthand for the phenomenon where, simply because an interest is shown, a response is obtained which might, but need not necessarily, have any relation to the *quality* of the interest. It is particularly likely to affect experiments with deprived children, starved of human communication, love and sympathy, who are suddenly made the focus of an experiment in which they are the principal actors.

On the other hand it might well be true, as the experimenters of this particular project argue, that the problems of helping deprived children are basically different from those affecting other, less culturally starved children, and that we ought not to think in terms of one kind of nursery-school environment, but of several different kinds, coping with children from different backgrounds. It might even be that for these children, whose whole mental development has lacked both discipline and variety, a type of rote learning might provide a stability that a more free approach does not, and that when we advocate free and creative play leading to concept formation and abstract thought, we ought first to define the kind of child who is likely to benefit from it and segregate out the child whose whole early history is so retarded that such an environment will simply precipitate mental confusion.

We have looked at three attempts to reinforce the intellectual development of the early years and inevitably they throw up more questions than answers. But they also indicate the immense amount of effort, of materials and of patience that is involved. While one might argue for one system or one theory against another, there can be little argument that such effort and such resources can rarely be found in even the best home environment. Again, one can be complacent and say that these kinds of effort, while they may be eminently worthwhile, are luxuries to which we must aspire rather than essentials for which we must strive. But we have our facts and they are uncompromising. What happens in the early years is irreversible. The luxury, one might almost conclude, is secondary education. It is the early years that count.

What is also striking, at this stage, is that so little work is being done to tackle some of the questions raised by these studies. In Britain not a single experimental pre-school group, whose object it is to try out different programmes of stimulus and response, exists. It is forty years since the Malting House first pointed the way to child development studies and pioneered a new approach to the pre-school child. The tragedy is that if Geoffrey Pyke were alive today and set up his school all over again, he would be nearly as far ahead of his time as he was in Cambridge in 1924. It was, after all, only a year or two ago that the Nuffield Foundation set aside a large sum of money to consider the introduction of science topics in the primary school, and articles are now being written about pioneering teachers who discuss problems of rust corrosion, of moths and larvae, or the germination of seeds with eight- and nine-year-olds.

By contrast, here is a description of an actual incident at the Malting House School.

David was sitting on his tricycle in the garden, back-pedalling. I said to him: 'You are not going forward, are you?'

He said: 'No, of course not, when I am turning them round the wrong way.'

I said to him: 'How does it go forward when it does? What makes it?'

He said, with a tone of scorn at my ignorance: 'Well, of course, your feet push the pedals round, and the pedals make that go round (pointing to the hub of the cranks) and that makes the chain go round, and the chain makes that go round (pointing to the hub of the wheel) and the wheels go round, and there you are.'

That conversation took place in 1927. David was five years old, and demonstrated that the understanding of casual relationships to fundamental to the appreciation of science, far from being the preserve of older children, can be developed in the young child.

Chapter Fourteen
The Needs of the Future

Jean Piaget, faced with summing up his life's researches on the mental development of young children, once put it this way: 'The more a child has seen and heard, the more he wants to see and hear.'

That brief statement might also serve as a summary of this book. I have tried to show that although we still know very little about the complicated processes that occur in childhood, we know enough to be concerned about the environment in which children develop. We can now see more clearly than was possible earlier how important it is that a young child should not simply get enough to eat and have room to move, toys to play with and a comfortable bed to sleep in, but that he should enjoy companionship and conversation, the stimulus of books and a multitude of play experiences, the stability of a good home and the opportunities to explore his environment so that he can build up, in his own mind, a working hypothesis of the world that enables him to move on to abstract thought.

We are not providing such an environment. In a survey carried out by the Central Office of Information for the Plowden Committee in 1964, it was found that of the 3237 parents questioned who had children at primary schools, 25 per cent lived in homes that could be classed as over-crowded (*Children and their Primary Schools*, vol. 2, app. 3, para. 2. 51). Seven per cent had no running water, 10 per cent had no fixed baths or showers, 13 per cent of the children played in streets that were not governed by any bye-laws forbidding traffic.

Moreover, many of our children do not enjoy a home that is intellectually stimulating. In this same survey more than half the parents had completed their own full-time formal education by the time they were fourteen, and 63 per cent of the fathers and 81 per cent of the mothers had themselves taken no further education courses once they had left school.

Less than half the parents belonged to a lending library and in approximately a third of the families neither parent had ever belonged to a library (para. 2. 19).

Nor are the homes in which our children grow up the kind of places in which the young can expect the attention they need. In 40 per cent of the families interviewed by the survey the mothers went out to work and we have seen that this is a growing trend. In 8 per cent of the families there existed the elements of a 'broken home' with either the father or the mother, or both, missing. About half the mothers interviewed admitted that they were too busy in the evenings to be available more than occasionally to read or play with their primary-school children, and a quarter of the fathers said that they were not able to join in activities with their children on week-day evenings. Almost a third went on to admit that they were only available occasionally, if at all, at week-ends.

I have tried to show, moreover, that even where the parents provide all the rudimentary essentials of a good child-orientated home and where pains are taken to give the child as rich and variegated an upbringing as possible, the rapacious mental hunger of the very young outstrips the ability of parents to provide for them sufficient stimulus and active encouragement; such an environment can only be provided by experienced teachers in a form of nursery school.

I have also tried to show that for a society committed to the ideal of equality of opportunity for all individuals, it is these young years that are the most crucial. Whatever remedial action we seek to take later – whether it takes the form of raising the school-leaving age, or a redistribution of wealth through taxation, or a more even spreading of welfare benefits, or a subsequent improvement in housing standards – whatever we do will amount to no more than sticking plaster on the initial wound. The damage – the irreversible damage – will have been done. No political policy can make an adult clever, or make him handle mathematical concepts, or improve his English, or qualify him for jobs that his educational standards do not allow him to take.

What we find, however, is that the present paucity of nursery-school places has become a weapon to increase the differentials between social classes. The government social survey shows that whereas 16 per cent of all parents interviewed had been able to send their child to either a nursery school or a nursery class before it attended primary school, the figure was substantially higher (25 per cent) among families with professional standing (*Children and their Primary Schools*, vol. 2, p. 136). These statistics take no account, of course, of the large number of private playgroups and nurseries run by middle-class parents and attended – if not exclusively, then certainly very largely – by children from their own social class.

What we find, therefore, is that in our adult world little thought is given to the needs of those young children who are asked to grow up in it. There are more by-laws that insist on a proper provision of parking space for cars than there are that demand proper areas of recreation and play for small children. Because no education authority has direct responsibility for their welfare, no representations are made on their behalf to any local planning committee. With the rapidly evolving environment brought about by the changing needs of a growing population and an advancing technology, with the development of television as a system of mass communication and the tendency for more mothers to go to work, with the increase in traffic and the need to create more and more homes in large tower blocks, this environment is becoming not merely unsatisfying but positively inimical to the needs of young children. And where provisions are made to alleviate this situation, the benefits appear to be seized by the very parents whose incomes, homes and educational background most qualify them for providing the essentials of their children's needs.

We need to become aware of these tendencies. We need to redress the balance. But it is not, of course, a phenomenon which is unique to England. Every modern, developing society can be accused of forgetting its young. Even in Sweden, often held up as an example of one of the most socially advanced European nations, only some 12·5 per cent of children between four and seven years of age – the starting age for formal schooling – can be given a place in kindergartens (Bruun, 1962,

1966). Many more are housed in either day nurseries or what are described as recreation nurseries, but neither of these institutions is primarily educational in intent, and their main aim is to look after children whose mothers are at work.

Russia, which has a pre-school child population of some 33,500,000, has made enormous strides in providing kindergartens for them. The need in the U.S.S.R. is particularly strong, because unlike Western European countries, almost 80 per cent of the women have jobs of some kind (*Women and Children in the U.S.S.R.: Brief Statistical Returns*, 1963, p. 77). Yet the number of places available for these children in kindergartens was, in 1961, only about 3,500,000, or some 10 per cent.

What is noticeable in a comparative study of pre-school provision is not that large differences exist between countries, but that a nation like Britain, which by common consent leads the world in the quality of its primary schools and the early age at which this education begins, lags behind when it comes to provision for the very young. France, where formal schooling begins at the age of six, has almost as many children between the ages of three and five as Britain. But in France, about 1,500,000 receive some sort of pre-schooling experience in *classes maternelles* or at special nursery schools, so that almost a quarter of the pre-school population is cared for in some way (*Informations Statistiques du Ministère de L'Education Nationale* Nos. 74–5, November 1965).

Perhaps the most dramatic recent attempt by any country to redress some of the inequalities arising out of a poor social environment has been the creation of the Headstart programme, within the wider context of the War on Poverty in the United States of America. This particular project is, frankly, a rescue operation aimed at giving children such as those we considered at Urbana (Chapter Thirteen) some sort of foretaste of the rudiments of learning. It is still too early to measure the success or the permanence of the Headstart programme, and it may well be that in the long term, the recent, less dramatic statement by the U.S. Educational Policies Commission, *Universal Opportunities of Early Child-*

hood Education, will be seen to have had a wider national impact.

The Commission, which is part of the National Education Association of the United States and the American Association of School Administrators, was emphatic about its views:

Research shows clearly that the first four or five years of a child's life is the period of most rapid growth in physical and mental characteristics and of greatest susceptibility to environmental influences. Consequently, it is in the early years that deprivations are most disastrous in their effects. They can be compensated for only with great difficulty in later years, and then probably not in full. Furthermore, it appears that it is harder to modify harmful learnings than to acquire new ones. Finally, experience indicates that exposure to a wide variety of activities and of social and mental interactions with children and adults greatly enhance a child's ability to learn. Few homes provide enough of these opportunities. It is reasonable to conclude that the postponement of an educational contribution by society until children reach the age of six [the starting age in the U.S.] generally limits the flowering of their potentials. (*Universal Opportunities of Early Childhood Education*, 1966, p. 3.)

The Commission went on to consider the importance of family life, and added: 'The need is for a complement, not an alternative, to family life. But the need is compelling.' It then pointed out that the need was most urgent among families already deprived, either in educational background, environment or economically.

But not only those commonly considered disadvantaged are disadvantaged in their lives at home. The pampered also are disadvantaged; so are those whose parents are obsessed with the need to impress and achieve; so are those, whatever their economic background, whose parents show them little love; so are those who have little chance to play with other children or with children of other backgrounds; so are those with physical handicaps. Early education could help all these children.

Early education is advisable for all children, not merely because of the need to offset any disadvantages in their background, but also because they are ready by the age of four for a planned fostering of their development and because educators know some of the ways to foster it through school programs. Early education has long been available to the well-to-do, and it is commendable that governments are now acting on the need to make it available to some of the poor. But the large middle group should have the same opportunities. (p. 4.)

The report (p. 5) concluded: 'The opportunity for early education at public expense should therefore be universal.'

Universal! Agreed. But in what form? Throughout this book, I have constantly referred to nursery education, not because nursery schools and kindergartens are necessarily the ideal forms, but because they provide a readily understood shorthand for the type of environment being advocated. Some teachers do in fact maintain that the nursery school, dealing exclusively with children from two to five, is the best solution to the environmental requirements of the very young. They argue that to a small child, another of six or seven appears as large and as dominating as an adult seems to the primary-school child, and that what is needed is a place apart where the small child feels under no threat, but secure, among children of his own age. But with those who passionately want to see public provision made for these children, there also lies the responsibility for advocating ways in which this can be done at a cost that is realistic. Is the cost of building separate nursery schools on their own sites, often away from the neighbourhood primary school where no land is available, a realistic policy, and is it, in the long run, in the interests of young children?

Although the Plowden Committee, in its recommendations about the extension of nursery schooling, was not specific on the matter, it appeared to favour the idea of separate facilities for nursery and infant schooling. If so, it differs from the view held by the U.S. Educational Policies Commission.

We think it important that the program for six-year-olds be based on the program for four- and five-year-olds. The need for this close association does not necessarily imply any one administrative structure. The early years could, for example, simply be attached to existing elementary schools, or a new school could be created to encompass the first four to eight years of education. However, the importance of continuity in the program suggests that it might be unwise to set off the first two years as a separate entity. (*Universal Opportunities of Early Childhood Education*, p. 11.)

This was also the view of the pioneers who ran the Malting House School and it is the hypothesis on which the Eveline Lowe School is based, both architecturally and intellectually. The evidence from schools such as these shows quite clearly that while young children have a need for a place where they can be isolated from the more aggressive, physically large and chronologically older children around them, they also derive a stimulus and, as their confidence grows, a sense of friendship from older children, some of whom might be their brothers and sisters.

To isolate these children and to treat them as in some way different in kind from those slightly older is not merely to create a totally false barrier around them, but also to isolate their teachers and their intellectual programme.

As we have seen, it was necessary to do this in the days when the elementary school provided a rigid, highly disciplined and unimaginative type of rote learning. This is no longer the case. Indeed, it is the reverse of the case.

What has therefore become possible is the emergence of a vastly more flexible attitude to the whole concept of schooling for young children. On the basis of the number of primary schools built between 1946 and 1965 in England and Wales – some 5000, or an average of 250 in any one year – it would be feasible to suggest that plans for new primary schools throughout the country should incorporate provisions for children from the age of three, along the lines of the Eveline Lowe School. If each of these 250 new schools were to take no more than eighty children who at present are not receiving any schooling (this is the number of under-fives going to Eveline Lowe), it would result in an annual increase of 20,000 places, purpose-built and under the direct jurisdiction of the Department of

Education, for children who at present are neglected. This would in a single year double the number of places at present available throughout the country in nursery schools. If the programme were to begin at once it would by the mid-seventies, when the Plowden Committee considered that is own recommendations could begin to take effect, have added a million places for these children at a cost per place no greater than that currently stipulated by the department.

The Plowden Committee was rightly most concerned to see pre-school places provided for children in what it termed educational priority areas. Inevitably, such a programme would have to make the best of the available resources, and in these cases separate nursery schools would almost certainly have to be provided. Such a programme is essential and its cost, at £3,000,000 a year, is not excessive. Indeed, measured in terms of the return, in the well-being of children, in their improvement in mental and physical health, and in their increased social maturity, the cost is negligible.

But a short-term 'rescue' programme for these areas must not be confused with the broader aim of providing a rich environment for all children at the age when they most need it. Obviously, this would be a slower process, but such is the inadequacy of the provision at the moment that, given the impetus, even a relatively modest programme over a fairly long period would make a considerable impact.

One of the stumbling blocks is, of course, the supply of teachers. No one can minimize this difficulty. But at the same time the problem need not be insuperable. The rash of play-groups that have been started throughout the country aptly demonstrates the enthusiasm of mothers who stand ready to help in any scheme which will further the development of their children. One of the nursery schools described in Chapter Eleven, which has a high reputation among professional educationists, makes extensive use of such assistants, welcomes their interest and considers their presence a positive virtue in establishing the home–school links that the Plowden Committee, too, recommend should be strengthened. Provided that the nursery classes of the primary schools were in the charge of a fully trained teacher, supported by possibly one or two trained assistants (and I do not necessarily mean three-year trained) there is no reason at all why they in turn should not be aided by parental help.

But the battle would be lost if we considered only the provision of nursery education, in whatever form. Ultimately, this is a discussion about the quality of our society. That quality will be only marginally improved if we limited our activities to providing special classes for the very young. For the question is much broader than that. What we need to ask ourselves is whether we are creating communities in which young children can grow up as free, enquiring, eager young people; whether, in visual, aesthetic, medical and intellectual terms we are providing for them the kind of environment which, ideally, we know they should have.

The answer will, in a society which is not rigidly controlled from above, always remain an approximation. So it should. We cannot expect all our park benches to be two foot high, or all our wash basins to be designed in such a way that young children can use them. The home and the community must reach a compromise between the needs of the very young, the adolescent, the adult, the aged and the handicapped. In our zeal to do right by young people, we cannot forget that their parents too need an environment that is specially shaped to their demands.

The point of this book is that no such compromise at present exists. The tragedy is that in forgetting about the four million of our citizens who will inherit our environment, we have not even succeeded in satisfying ourselves. Our cities are clogged, our air begrimed, our rivers polluted. Our suburbs are cultural deserts. Our public buildings are hideous and our ability to communicate with our neighbours grows daily more difficult. There is evidence that our class divisions are growing and that the rift between our affluent communities and the under-developed areas of our economy are becoming more severe. We preach equality of opportunity but we beget segregation and discrimination. We preach beauty and create monstrous ugliness. We ought to be angry about it; instead we become complacent.

But if we are complacent about our own condition, we have

no right to be complacent about the world our children inherit, nor about the future they will create. For when we plead for the fullest possible education of the young, we do so not merely because it is their birthright, or because they are small and defenceless, or because it is the most effective means of making our education system an efficient one. It is a plea, rather, for the future. If we possess the knowledge that will prevent delinquency, frustration and misery, have we the right not to exercise the power which that knowledge provides? If we can do better by all children, can we sit back and not act? These are questions that deal, not with education, but with the very purposes of civilization. They were asked by Pastor Witte in 1800, by Robert Owen in 1816, by the McMillen sisters in 1920, by the authors of the Committee of Enquiry in 1929. They are implied by the Plowden Report of 1967. And they have not had an answer.

Appendix

Ministry of Education Circular 8/60 on Nursery Education[1]

Nursery Education

I Introduction

1   There is no change in the circumstances which have made it impossible to undertake any expansion in the provision of nursery education. The Minister wishes, however, to consolidate the current guidance on this subject and to bring it up to date, especially in view of the recent development of part-time education. Circulars 175, 202, 280 and 313, Administrative Memoranda Nos. 103, 120 and 129, and paragraph 17 of Circular 350, are cancelled.

2   The attention of authorities is drawn to the definition of 'nursery class' in Regulation 3(1) of the Schools Regulations, 1959, as 'a class mainly for children who have attained the age of three years but have not attained the age of five years.' The provisions of this circular apply to all such classes, whether or not they were regarded as nursery classes before the coming into operation of these regulations.

II Policy

3   Authorities are required by Section 8(2)(b) of the Education Act, 1944, to have regard 'to the need for securing that provision is made for pupils who have not attained the age of five years by the provision of nursery schools or, where the authority consider the provision of such schools to be inexpedient, by the provision of nursery classes in other schools.' It has not, however, at any time since the Act came into operation been possible to undertake any expansion in the provision of nursery education.

4   The White Paper on *Secondary Education for All* issued in December, 1958, announced a five-year programme devoted principally to the improvement of secondary education and also emphasized the urgent need to reduce the size of classes in both primary and secondary schools. No resources can at present be spared for the expansion of nursery education and in particular no teachers can be spared who might otherwise work with children of compulsory school age.

1. Sent to L.E.A.s on 31 May 1960.

5   At the same time the Minister values the excellent work being done in nursery schools and classes, and is anxious to ensure its continuance, both for its own sake and as a base for expansion in the future when the time comes for a full application of the principles set out in the 1944 Act. He believes therefore that authorities will best carry out their statutory responsibilities at the present time by maintaining the provision of nursery education at its present level wherever conditions are satisfactory, by securing advances in the already high quality of the service and in the effective use of current resources.

6   Thus the Minister cannot encourage authorities to propose any new nursery schools, except by way of replacement where existing buildings have to be taken out of use, or any enlargement of nursery schools which would require increased staff according to the standards set out in part IV of this circular; but equally he would deprecate any proposal to discontinue an existing school working in satisfactory conditions and meeting a clear need.

7   In the case of nursery classes the Minister is especially concerned to ensure that teachers are not diverted from the teaching of older children. There may be infant schools with declining numbers of pupils which find themselves with spare accommodation which would be suitable for nursery classes and it may appear that such classes could be satisfactorily staffed. The Minister is convinced, however, that over the whole area of an authority any net increase in the number of pupils under compulsory school age must, if adequate staff is provided, reduce the supply of teachers available for older children. He must, therefore, ask authorities, in consultation where necessary with voluntary school managers, to continue to restrict the number of such pupils, in their respective areas as a whole, within present limits. He will expect the total number of pupils under five, excluding those who will reach the age of five during their first term at school, in the schools (other than nursery schools) maintained by each authority not to exceed the corresponding number at the same time of year in the educational year 1956–1957. For this purpose, two part-time pupils in a two-shift nursery class (see part III of this Circular) will count as one full-time pupil.

III   Part-Time Nursery Education

8   During and immediately after the war one of the main purposes served by nursery schools and classes was to release mothers of

young children for work of national importance. To serve this purpose it was necessary for nursery education to be full-time.

9   The Minister believes that it is now widely understood that nursery education, in common with all primary and secondary education of which it forms a part, is provided in the interests of the children. The aim is always to meet the needs of the particular child.

10   It is arguable that the needs of normal children under five years old, coming from normal homes, are more likely to be for part-time than for full-time education. With this in mind, a number of authorities have for several years organized some of their nursery schools and classes wholly or partly on a two-shift basis. Those children who attend only in the mornings are balanced by an equal number who attend only in the afternoons; and none of these children has a midday meal at school. In a nursery school there may, or may not, be others who attend in both the mornings and the afternoons and have their midday meals at school; but such an arrangement may present difficulties in a nursery class unless two separate rooms are available.

11   These arrangements were made in the first place as experiments, but they have proved very successful and are now firmly established in a number of places. The Minister feels that the time has now come to bring the possibility to the attention of authorities generally and to encourage them to consider whether to introduce similar arrangements in some of their nursery schools and classes where conditions are suitable. The Minister would be glad to be informed of any such proposal and H.M. Inspectors will always be ready to advise authorities in the light of the experience already gained.

12   The advantages of such arrangements are easily seen. At best, the effect is to provide, without any additional staff, accommodation or expense, a better introduction to school life for twice the number of children. The Minister is particularly attracted by the possibility which is opened of providing appropriate nursery education for children from normal homes, who have so often in the past had to yield to children in difficult circumstances for medical or social reasons.

13   At the same time, two warnings are necessary. One is that not all needs can be met by part-time attendance. Children in difficult circumstances must continue to receive special consideration. Some

of them may be suited just as well, or even better, by part-time attendance; but there will be others who need a full day at school. Some mothers are forced by circumstances to do a full day's work away from home; and there are districts in which the tradition of the full-time working mother is so strong that any diminution in the provision of full-time nursery education could only be undertaken with caution. The Minister recognizes therefore that full-time nursery education will have to continue on a substantial scale; he asks only that authorities should question its extent and keep in mind the possible alternatives.

14   The other necessary warning is that there should be no additional or wasteful use of staff. Part-time facilities can be introduced only to replace, directly or indirectly, existing full-time facilities; this is no exception to the rule set out in part II of this circular that no expansion can at present be contemplated. In this connexion authorities may care to know that schools offering part-time facilities have not been embarrassed by any strong parental preference for morning rather than afternoon attendance.

IV   Staffing

15   The Minister's requirements are set out in Regulation 16 of the Schools Regulations, 1959. This part of the Circular explains more precisely what the Minister regards as a suitable and sufficient staff of teachers under paragraph 1 of the regulations and in what circumstances he considers that a person who is not a qualified teacher may be appointed to a nursery school or class under paragraph 3(c) of the regulation.

16   Every *nursery school* must have a qualified superintendent teacher. Including the superintendent, the Minister regards as a suitable and sufficient staff for a nursery school one teacher and the equivalent of one full-time nursery assistant for every twenty full-time or forty part-time pupils. Authorities will no doubt continue to bear in mind the need to limit the size of the groups in which young children spend their school day; the Minister would think it reasonable if they continued to regard the equivalent of forty full-time pupils as the normal size of nursery school and, where larger numbers are necessary, to ensure that they are dispersed in smaller self-contained groups.

17   For a *nursery class* the Minister regards as a suitable and sufficient staff one teacher and the equivalent of one full-time nursery assistant. Under Regulation 6 of the Schools Regulations,

1959, the number of pupils in a nursery class may not exceed thirty; this limit should be strictly observed, as the Minister does not consider in the case of a nursery class that a higher number of full-time pupils (though for this purpose two part-time pupils may be counted as one full-time pupil) could be justified under the terms of the proviso to this regulation.

18   Both in nursery schools and in nursery classes, two nursery students may reasonably take the place of one nursery assistant.

19   The Minister holds strongly that in the long run all teachers in nursery schools and classes should be qualified. During the present shortage of teachers, however, he regards it as inevitable, and has accepted in Regulation 16(3)(c) of the Schools Regulations, that some teachers in charge of nursery classes and assistant teachers in nursery schools should have no teaching qualifications. The regulation provides that such a teacher must have 'completed a course of instruction in the care of young children' and the Minister would regard this condition as satisfied if she held the certificate of the National Nursery Examination Board and had in addition, after a period of experience in nursery work, taken a refresher course provided by a local education authority to fit her for added responsibilities.

20   The Minister's regulations make no requirements as to the qualifications of nursery assistants. He would expect, however, that authorities will normally confine new appointments to holders of the certificate of the National Nursery Examination Board. Nursery assistants possessing this or an equivalent qualification should be paid as Nursery Assistants Class I on the Whitley Council scale. Nursery Assistants not possessing this qualification, whether already in employment or appointed exceptionally in future, should normally be paid as Nursery Assistants Class II on the Whitley Council scale.

Addendum No. 1 to Circular 8/60 (7 July 1964)

1   Ministry of Education Circular 8/60 set out the considerations, notably the shortage of teachers, which made it necessary to hold the provision of nursery schools and classes broadly at the existing level.

2   These considerations are still valid; in particular the renewed rise in the number of children reaching school age is already confronting the primary schools with staffing problems which are likely to grow more serious over the next few years. The general

restriction on expansion of nursery provision must, therefore, remain. The Secretary of State recognizes, however, that in some cases the establishment of new nursery provision, by enabling qualified women with young children to teach in maintained schools, may produce a net increase in teaching strength. Accordingly, while he has no wish to persuade mothers of young children to undertake teaching service sooner than they themselves think right in relation to their children's development and family commitments, the Secretary of State will welcome limited exceptions to the general policy, where an authority is satisfied that a pool of qualified women exists who wish to undertake such service but are prevented from doing so only by the absence of nursery provision for their children.

3 If such extensions to existing nursery provision are not to result in a deterioration of staffing standards in tother schools, it will be essential that local education authorities should exercise careful judgement in every case where they propose to implement arrangements of this kind. In particular the following conditions should apply:

(a) The new provision should be in nursery classes. It would not normally be appropriate to build new or extend existing nursery schools for this purpose, since they generally require purpose-built accommodation and a higher teacher/pupil ratio. Nursery classes may be full-time or part-time;

(b) Suitable accommodation should be already available; the cost of any minor building work will fall to be met from the current allocation;

(c) The authority should be able to identify in advance an appreciable number of qualified women teachers who will both send their children to the new nursery class and teach in a school maintained by them or by another authority;

(d) Though admissions need not be restricted to the children of women teachers, the authority should be ready to give such children priority for admission over other applications;

(e) The authority should keep under review the extent to which the new class continues to serve its prime purpose of securing an appreciable net increase in the maintained school teaching force.

4 The Secretary of State does not require proposals to establish new nursery classes under this addendum to be submitted in advance for his approval, but authorities are asked to inform him when such classes are established, giving for each class

(i) the date, (ii) the school, and (iii) the number of teachers whom it will bring into service in the first instance, divided into full- and part-time teachers, and into teachers in primary and in secondary schools,
and to bring the figure at (iii) up to date at the beginning of each subsequent year.

Addendum No. 2 to Circular 8/60 (3 December 1965)

1   The Secretary of State has recently reviewed the operation of Addendum No. 1 which was issued on 7 July 1964. In the light of this review, he believes that a further controlled expansion of nursery facilities should be encouraged where this will increase the return to service of married women teachers or facilitate the recruitment of married women graduates who have never taught before, and he has accordingly decided to introduce more flexible arrangements to achieve this end. This Addendum, which supersedes Addendum No. 1, sets out these new arrangements.

A New Approach

2   The review referred to above has shown that, although only a few local education authorities have so far made use of the concession offered in Addendum No. 1, more of them are now planning to do so. The Secretary of State accordingly proposes to retain, as one method by which a local education authority may justify the establishment of new nursery facilities, the method previously set out in Addendum No. 1, modified only by a more precise definition of its requirements. This method, as modified, is subsequently referred to as Method 1.

3   The review has also established, however, that the existing system of nursery schools and classes already produces more teachers than it consumes, i.e. that the number of qualified women teachers whose service in maintained schools is facilitated by their children's attendance at maintained nursery schools or classes exceeds the number of teachers who are employed in the maintained nursery system. The Secretary of State has therefore decided that he can also offer an alternative method, subsequently referred to as Method 2, by which an authority may justify the establishment of new nursery facilities. For this purpose, the criterion to be used under Method 2 is not the number of teachers whose return to service would result from the establishment of a particular class, but rather the extent to which the authority's nursery provision as a whole already enables – and would continue to enable – qualified women teachers to give service in maintained schools.

Requirements

4   Subject to the other provisions of this Addendum and, in particular, to the conditions set out in paragraph 6 below, the requirements of these two methods are as follows:

(a)   Method 1. In advance of establishing any additional nursery provision, an authority shall identify four[1] qualified women teachers[2] who will place their children in the proposed nursery class and will teach in schools maintained by local education authorities. An authority now maintaining fewer than three nursery classes (whether in nursery schools or in primary schools) must satisfy the requirements of Method 1 in order to establish additional nursery classes until their provision reaches this total. An authority operating three or more classes (whether existing classes or those set up under Method 1) may establish further nursery facilities either by the use of Method 1, or, if the necessary conditions are fulfilled, in accordance with Method 2.

(b)   Method 2. Before this method may be used, an authority's nursery provision must consist of at least three classes which are currently securing the release for service in maintained schools of at least twelve[1] qualified women teachers. Where these conditions are satisfied, an authority may establish additional nursery facilities provided that, after their establishment, the number[1] of qualified women teachers whose service in maintained schools is facilitated by their children's attendance at any of the authority's nursery schools or classes remains at least twice the number of teachers who are employed in the authority's nursery schools and classes as a whole (not counting nursery assistants employed in charge of nursery classes under Regulation 16(3)(c) of the Schools Regulations, 1959 – see paragraphs 11 and 12 below).

5   This scheme contains an incentive element. Provided an authority already maintain, or can build up under Method 1, at least three classes which currently enable at least twelve[1] qualified women teachers to give service in maintained schools, they may extend their nursery provision within the limits indicated in Method 2, subject to the other conditions described in this Addendum. For example, an authority maintaining three classes which employed three nursery teachers and released twelve qualified teachers for service could establish up to three additional

---

1. Including part-time teachers at their full-time equivalent value.
2. Throughout this Addendum the phrase 'qualified women teachers' includes women graduates who have never taught before.

classes. The authority would not, of course, be obliged to establish so many extra classes and should not do so unless reasonably confident that the classes would continue to justify themselves in terms of additional teachers released for service. In making arrangements under the Addendum, authorities are asked to bear in mind the over-riding need to avoid prejudicing the staffing of schools for children of statutory school age; the ratio of two teachers released for service in maintained schools to every one employed in nursery education is regarded as a minimum safety margin. Temporary fluctuations below this ratio will not require the closure of classes already established, but any further expansion of facilities will obviously depend upon a sufficient improvement in the ratio for the requirements of Method 2 to be satisfied.

General Conditions to be Observed

6   The following general conditions will apply to the establishment of additional nursery facilities:

(a)   Although admissions need not be restricted to the children of women teachers, the authority should give such children priority for admission to a nursery class set up under Method 1, or throughout their nursery provision if Method 2 is adopted;

(b)   The additional facilities may be full-time or part-time and should normally be in the form of nursery classes to be housed in existing school accommodation which is suitable or can be adapted for the purpose; but the provisions of this Addendum may be held also to apply where:

  (i)   existing accommodation is available which can be adapted at a minimum cost for use as a nursery school; or

  (ii)   the authority can hire suitable accommodation in premises where a nursery class can be adequately supervised from a nearby primary school;

(c)   The cost of any minor building work will fall to be met from the authority's current allocation;

(d)   The suitability of accommodation for nursery use should be discussed with H.M. Inspector.

7   Authorities are asked to refer in advance to the Department any proposal to set up a new nursery school under the terms of this Addendum. They are free to set up other nursery facilities under this Addendum without prior consultation.

Annual Review of the Arrangements

8   All authorities maintaining nursery facilities, whether or not

these include facilities set up under the terms of this Addendum or of Addendum No. 1, are asked to keep under review the extent to which their nursery provision as a whole both employs teachers and releases women teachers for service, and to make an annual return of this information to the Department in January of each year. Authorities will be notified of the exact form in which this information will be sought.

General Observations

9   The Secretary of State is aware that there may sometimes appear to be a conflict between the need to release married women teachers for service and the need to maintain standards in nursery education; and he wishes to reaffirm that nursery education is primarily designed for the benefit of children and is only secondarily of value in helping to promote the return to service of married women teachers. He would not wish, therefore, to urge local education authorities to adopt arrangements in pursuit of the second aim which would prejudice the achievement of the first – arrangements, for example, which involved children in excessively long journeys to and from a nursery or in separation from their mothers for excessively long hours. Neither would he wish to persuade mothers with young children to resume teaching before they themselves thought it right to do so. For his part, he would think that the provision of part-time nursery facilities, coupled with opportunities for part-time employment in the schools, might often be the arrangement which would best serve the interests of both the children and of their teacher-mothers.

Priority for Teachers' Children

10   The survey of nursery provision has shown that, in general, the nursery facilities maintained by authorities who give priority of admission to teachers' children produce proportionately twice as many returning teachers as the facilities provided by authorities not giving this priority. To offer priority of admission to teachers' children is clearly, then, expedient; but in return for operating this policy, an authority may well, under the arrangements announced above, be able also to offer some more nursery places to other children, which they could not otherwise have done.

The Use of Nursery Assistants

11   It was acknowledged in paragraph 19 of Circular 8/60 that the employment in nursery schools and classes of suitably qualified nursery assistants in charge of classes under the terms of

Regulation 16(3)(c) of the Schools Regulations, 1959 was an expedient made necessary by the shortage of qualified teachers. Today, acute teacher shortage still persists; and the nursery system, partly dependent upon these nursery assistants for its staffing, is helping to speed up the return flow of qualified women teachers to the schools and is thus, in some measure, alleviating that shortage. In these circumstances, the Secretary of State thinks it right that authorities should continue, where necessary, to employ nursery assistants on this footing.

12   Those selected for employment on such duties should, of course, be the best qualified and most experienced nursery assistants available, and they should be given opportunities to attend refresher courses designed to fit them for these added responsibilities. All authorities employing nursery assistants in charge of classes, and especially those who do so on a substantial scale, should satisfy themselves that they employ sufficient qualified teachers with specialist nursery training to sustain the best practice of nursery education throughout their nursery provision as a whole, and that these teachers are conveniently available to offer nursery assistants in charge of classes any necessary support. Subject to the same safeguards, other authorities could usefully consider whether additional nursery facilities, if otherwise practicable, might be staffed on this basis where additional qualified nursery teachers are not available.

The Use of other Methods

13   The Secretary of State would expect authorities to adopt one or other of the methods described in this Addendum wherever it was possible for them to do so. There may be a few areas, however, where local circumstances are such that neither method would be effective. Authorities in this situation who believe that they could secure a net increase in the teacher force through the expansion of their nursery provision by some other method consistent with the spirit of this Addendum, are invited to submit their proposals to the Department for consideration.

References

Adams, F. J., Millar, E. L. M., Jefferys, M., and Van der Eyken, W. (1968), *New Opportunities for Young Children*, Nursery Schools Association.

Adamson, G. (1968), 'Should foster mums be paid?', *New Society*, 22 August 1968, pp. 268–9.

Alexander, T., Stoyle, J., and Kirk, C. (1968), 'The language of children in the "inner city"', *J. Psychol.*, vol. 68, pp. 215–21.

Allen, K. E., Hart, B. M., Buell, J. S., Harris, F. R., and Wolf, M. M. (1964), 'Effects of social reinforcement on isolate behaviour of a nursery school child', *Child Dev.*, vol. 35, pp. 511–18.

Axtell, J. B., and Edmunds, M. W. (1960), 'The effects of pre-school experience on fathers, mothers and children', *California J. educ. Res.*, pp. 195–203.

Baldwin, A. L. (1949), 'The effect of home environment on nursery school behaviour', *Child Dev.*, vol. 20, pp. 49–62.

Baldwin, C. M. (1963), 'The role of verbal interaction on the cognitive development of pre-school children', *Paper Presented to Conference on Improvement of Nursery School Curriculum*, May 1963.

Barrett, H. E., and Koch, H. L. (1930), 'The effects of nursery school training on the mental test performance of a group of orphanage children', *J. genet. Psychol.*, vol. 37, pp. 102–22.

Bereiter, C., Engelman, S., Osborn, J., and Redford, P. (1966), 'An academically oriented pre-school for culturally deprived children', in F. M. Hechinger (ed.), *Pre-School Education Today*, Doubleday.

Bernstein, B. (1961), 'Social class and linguistic development: A theory of social learning', in A. H. Halsey, J. Floud and C. A. Anderson (ed.), *Education, Economy and Society*, Free Press of Glencoe.

Biber, B. (1964), 'Pre-school education', in R. Ulrich (ed.), *Education and the Idea of Mankind*, Council for the Study of Mankind, Harcourt Brace.

Biber, B., and **Franklin, M. B.** (1967), 'The relevance of developmental and psychodynamic concepts to the education of the pre-school child', *J. of the Amer. Acad. child Psychiat.*, vol. 6, no. 1.

Biber, B., and **Minuchin, P.** (1968), 'A child development approach to language in the pre-school disadvantaged child', in *Monog. Soc. Res. Child Devel.*, vol. 33, no. 8.

Bloom, B. (1964), *Stability and Change in Human Characteristics*, Wiley.

Blyth, W. A. C. (1968), *English Primary Education, Vols. 1 and 2*, Routledge & Kegan Paul.

Booney, M. E., and **Nicholson, E. L.** (1958), 'Comparative social adjustments of elementary school pupils with and without pre-school training', *Child Dev.*, vol. 19, pp. 125–33.

Bowlby, J. (1964), *Child Care and the Growth of Love*, Penguin Books.

Boyce, A. J. (1968), 'The how and why of human diversity', *New Society*, 18 July 1968, pp. 128–30.

Brain–hormone Relationship, Current Medical Research, H.M.S.O., 1968.

Brook, D. (1966), 'Hertford's new nursery school', *Maternal and Child Care*, January 1966, pp. 13–16.

Bruun, Y. (1962), *Nursery Schools in Sweden*, Swedish Institute, Stockholm; (1962), *Supplementary Information*, Swedish Institute.

Building for Nursery Education, Department of Education and Science, Architect's and Building Branch, Design Note 1, 1968.

Caldwell, E., and **Hall, V. C.** (1968), 'Concept learning in discrimination tasks', in *Final Report, Project Headstart Research and Evaluation Center, Syracuse University*.

Calveley, A. (1962), *Starting a Community Nursery School*, Nursery School Association, no. 73.

Campbell-Smith, N., and **McFarland, M.** (1963), 'The role of the nursery teacher in the development of child personality', *J. nurs. Educ.*, vol. 19, pp. 5–18.

The Case for Nursery Schools. Education Enquiry Committee Report, Philips, 1929.

Casler, L. (1965), 'The effect of supplementary verbal stimulation on a group of institutionalized infants', *J. child Psychol. Psychiat.,* vol. 6, pp. 19–27.

Children and their Primary Schools, Report of the Central Advisory Council of Education (England), 2 vols, H.M.S.O., 1967. (Plowden Report.)

Children in Care in England and Wales. March 1967, Home Office, H.M.S.O., Commd. 3514. 1968.

Christianson, H. M., Rogers, M. M., and **Ludlum, B. A.** (1961), *The Nursery School: Adventure in Living and Learning,* Houghton Mifflin.

Churchill, E. M. (1962), *Piaget's Findings and the Teacher,* National Froebel Foundation.

Circular 8/60, Department of Education and Science, May 1960; *Addendum 1 to Circular 8/60,* July 1964; *Addendum 2 to Circular 8/60,* December 1965. [See Appendix.]

Circumstances of Families, Ministry of Social Security, H.M.S.O., 1967.

Clarke, M. (1968), Success before six?, *Trends in Education,* H.M.S.O.

Clegg, A. (1966), 'The twilight children', *Where ?,* Advisory Centre for Education.

Clegg, A., and **Megson, B.** (1968), *Children in Distress,* Penguin Education.

Coombs, P. H. (1968), *The World Educational Crisis. A Systems Analysis,* Oxford University Press.

Coopersmith, S. (ed.) (1966), *Frontiers of Psychological Research,* W. H. Freeman & Co.

Cowley, J. J., and **Griesel, R. D.** (1966), *Animal Behaviour,* vol. 14, part 4.

Crosland, A. (1956), *The Future of Socialism*, Cape.

Cushing, H. M. (1934), 'A tentative report on the influence of nursery school training upon kindergarten adjustment as reported by kindergarten teachers', *Child Dev.*, vol. 5, pp. 304–14.

Davis, A. (1961), *Social-Class Influences Upon Learning*, Harvard University Press.

Dawe, H. C. (1942), 'A study of the effect of an educational program upon language development and related mental functions in young children', *J. exp. Educ.*, vol. 11, pp. 200–209.

Denenberg, V. H. (1964), 'Critical periods, stimulus input and emotional reactivity: A theory of infantile stimulation', *Psychol. Rev.*, vol. 71, pp. 335–51.

Dennis, W. (1935), 'The effect of restricted practice upon the reaching, sitting and standing of two infants', *J. genet. Psychol.*, vol. 47, pp. 17–32.

Dennis, W., and **Sayegh, Y.** (1965), 'The effects of supplementary experiences upon the behavioural development of infants in institutions', *Child Dev.*, vol. 36, pp. 81–90.

Deutsch, M. (1963), 'The disadvantaged child and the learning process', in A. H. Passow (ed.), *Education in Depressed Areas*, Bureau of Publications, Teachers College, Columbia University.

Doman, G. J., Stevens, G. L., and **Orem, R. C.** (1964), *How to Teach Your Baby to Read: The Gentle Revolution*, Random House.

Douglas, J. W. B. (1964), *The Home and the School*, MacGibbon & Kee.

Douglas, J. W. B., and **Blomfield, J. M.** (1958), *Children Under Five*, Institute of Child Health, University of London.

Douglas, J. W. B., and **Ross, J. M.** (1964), 'The later educational progress and emotional adjustment of children who went to nursery school or classes', *Educ. Res.*, vol. 7, p. 73.

Douglas, J. W. B., Ross, J. M., and **Simpson, H. R.** (1968), *All Our Future*, Peter Davies.

Dubin, E. R. (1946), 'The effect of training on the tempo of development of graphic representation in pre-school children', *J. exp. Educ.*, vol. 15, pp. 166–73.

Dinnage, R., and **Kellmer Pringle, M. L.** (1967), *Foster Home Care – Facts and Fallacies,* Longmans.

Dinnage, R., and **Kellmer Pringle, M. L.** (1967), *Residential Child Care – Facts and Fallacies,* Longmans.

Ellingson, R. J. (1964), 'Studies of electrical activity of the developing human brain', in W. A. Hamwich and H. E. Hamwich (eds.), *The Developing Brain, Progress in Brain Research,* vol. 9, Elsevier.

Feldman, S. (1964), 'A pre-school enrichment program for disadvantaged children', *New Era,* vol. 45, pp. 79–82.

Fogg, G. E. (1963), *The Growth of Plants,* Penguin Books.

Fowler, W. (1961), 'Cognitive stimulation, I.Q. changes, and cognitive learning in three-year-old identical twins and triplets', *Amer. Psychol.,* vol. 16, p. 373.

Galambos, R. (1967), 'Electrical events in the brain and learning', in D. B. Lindsley and A. A. Lumsdaine (eds.), *Brain Function and Learning, UCLA Forum in Medical Sciences,* vol. 4, University of California Press.

Gardner, D. B., Hawkes, G. R., and **Burchinal, L. G.** (1961), 'Noncontinuous mothering in infancy and development in later childhood', *Child Dev.,* vol. 32, pp. 225–34.

Geraghty, T. (1966), 'Drama without end in these thirteen storeys', *Guardian,* 10 October 1966.

Gesell, A. (1930), *The Mental Growth of the Pre-school Child,* Macmillan.

Goldfarb, W. (1943), 'The effects of early institutional care on adolescent personality', *J. exp. Educ.,* vol. 12, pp. 106–29.

Gordon, E. W. (1965), 'A review of programs of compensatory education', *Amer. J. Orthopsychiat.,* vol. 35, pp. 640–51.

Gordon, I. J. (ed.) (1965), *Human Development. Readings in Research,* Scott, Foreman & Co.

Gray, P. H. (1958), 'Theory and evidence of imprinting in human infants', *J. Psychol.,* vol. 46, pp. 155–66.

Gray, S. W., and **Klaus, R. A.** (1965), 'An experimental pre-school program for culturally deprived children', *Child Dev.,* vol. 36, pp. 887–98.

Greene, K. B. (1931), 'Relations between kindergartens and nursery schools', *Childhood Educ.*, vol. 8, pp. 352–5.

Gregory, E. (1968), 'The child-minding tangle', *New Society*, 8 February 1968, pp. 196–7.

Griffiths, A. N. (1939), Intelligence and certain personality traits of twenty-four children who have attended Iowa State College Nursery School, *Master's Thesis, Iowa State College.*

Griffiths, R. (1954), *The Abilities of Babies*, University of London Press.

Hall, V. C., and **Caldwell, E.** (1968), 'Discrimination of letter-like forms', in *Final Report. Project Headstart Research and Evaluation Center, Syracuse University.*

Harlow, H. F., and **Kuenne, M.** (1949), 'Learning to think', *Scient. Amer.*, August.

Harris, F. R., Johnston, M. K., Kelley, C. S., and **Wolf, M. M.** (1964), 'Effects of positive social reinforcement on regressed crawling of a nursery school child', *J. educ. Psychol.*

Harrold, M. V., and **Temple, M. H.** (1959–60), A study of children in the admission classes of four infant schools, making a comparison between those who have attended a nursery school and those admitted direct from home, *Unpublished Thesis. Child Development Centre, Institute of Education, University of London.*

Hartley, R. E., Frank, L. K., and **Goldenson, R. M.** (1952), *Understanding Children's Play*, Columbia University Press.

Hartup, W. W., and **Keller, E. D.** (1960), 'Nurturance in pre-school children in its relation to dependency', *Child Dev.*, vol. 31, pp. 681–9.

Hattwick, B. W. (1936), 'The influence of nursery attendance upon the behaviour and personality of the pre-school child', *J. exper. Educ.*, vol. 5, pp. 180–90.

Heafford, M. R. (1967), *Pestalozzi*, Methuen.

Heathers, G. (1955), 'Emotional dependence and independence in nursery school play', *J. genet. Psychol.*, vol. 87, pp. 37–57.

Hebb, D. O. (1947), 'The effects of early experience on problem-solving at maturity', *Amer. Psychol.*, vol. 2, pp. 306–7.

Hechinger, F. M. (ed.) (1966), *Pre-School Education Today*, Doubleday.

Hess, R. P., and **Bear, R. Meyer** (1968), *Early Education. Current Theory, Research and Practice*, Aldine Publishing Co.

Highberger, R. (1955), 'The relationship between maternal behaviour and the child's early adjustment to nursery school', *Child Dev.*, vol. 26, pp. 49–61.

Hilgard, J. R. (1932), 'Learning and maturation in pre-school children', *J. genet. Psychol.*, vol. 41, pp. 31–56.

Hoffman, M. L., and **Hoffman, L. W.** (eds.) (1964, 1967), *Review of Child Development Research. Vols. 1 and 2*, Russell Sage Foundation, New York.

Hole, V. (1966), Children's play on housing estates, *Ministry of Technology Building Research Station. National Building Studies. Research Paper*, no. 39, H.M.S.O.

Homes for Today and Tomorrow, Ministry of Housing and Local Government, 1961.

Honzik, M. P., Macfarlane, J. W., and **Allen, L.** (1948), 'The stability of mental test performance between two and eighteen years', *J. exp. Educ.*, vol. 17, pp. 309–24.

Horowitz, F. D. (1962), 'Incentive value of social stimuli for pre-school children', *Child Dev.*, vol. 33, pp. 111–16.

Household Composition Tables, Census 1961, H.M.S.O., 1966.

Howe, E. (1966), *Under Five: A Report on Nursery Education*, Conservative Political Centre.

Hubel, D. H., and **Weisel, T. N.** (1963), *J. Neurol. Physiol.* vol. 26.

Hunt, A. (1968), *A Survey of Women's Employment*, Government Social Survey, H.M.S.O.

Hunt, J. McVicker (1961), *Intelligence and Experience*, Ronald Press.

Hunt, J. McVicker (1964), 'The psychological basis for using pre-school enrichment as an antidote for cultural deprivation', *Merrill–Palmer Quarterly*, vol. 10, pp. 209–48.

Hurtwood, Lady Allen (1968), *Planning for Play*, Thames & Hudson.

Illingworth, R. S. (1966), *The Development of the Infant and the Young Child: Normal and Abnormal*, Livingstone.

Informations Statistiques du Ministère de L'Education National, nos. 74–5, November 1965.

Isaacs, N. (1961), *The Growth of Understanding in the Young Child*, Educational Supply Association.

Isaacs, S. (1931), *Intellectual Growth in Young Children*, Routledge.

Isaacs, S. (1933), *Social Development in Young Children*, Routledge.

Isaacs, S. (1948), *Childhood and After*, Routledge & Kegan Paul.

Jahoda, M., and **Warren, N.** (1968), 'Intelligence – Nature and Nurture', *New Scientist*, 25 July 1968, pp. 188–90.

Jensen, A. R. (1963), 'Learning ability in retarded, average and gifted children', *Merrill–Palmer Quarterly*, vol. 9, pp. 123–40.

Jersild, A. T., and **Fite, M. D.** (1939), 'The influence of nursery school experience on children's social adjustment', *Child Dev.*, monograph 5, Teachers College, Columbia University.

Jersild, A. T., and **Bienstock, S. F.** (1931), 'The influence of training on the vocal ability of three-year-old children', *Child Dev.*, vol. 2, pp. 272–91.

Joel, W. (1939), 'The influence of nursery school education upon behaviour maturity', *J. exper. Educ.*, vol. 8, pp. 164–5.

Johnston, M. K., Kelly, C. S., Harris, F. R., and **Wolf, M. M.** (1966), 'An application of reinforcement principles to development of motor skills of a young child', *Child Dev.*, vol. 37, pp. 379–87.

Kahan, B. (1968), 'Children "in care"', *New Society*, 2 May 1968, p. 643.

Kawin, E., and **Hoefer, C.** (1931), *A Comparative Study of a Nursery School versus a Non-nursery School Group*, University of Chicago Press.

Keeley, B. (ed.) (1968), *1020 Playgroups*, Pre-school Playgroup Association.

Klatskin, E. H. (1952), 'Intelligence test performance at one year among infants raised with flexible methodology', *J. clin. Psychol.*, vol. 8, pp. 230–37.

Klineberg, O. (1963), 'Negro–White differences in intelligence test performance: A new look at an old problem', *Amer. Psychol.*, vol. 18, pp. 198–203.

Lampe, D. (1959), *Pyke: The Unknown Genius*, Evans.

Lamson, E. C. (1940), 'A follow-up study of a group of nursery school children', in *Yearbook Nat. Soc. Studies Educ.*, part 2, pp. 231–6.

Lapping, A. (1969), 'London against Seebohm', *New Society*, 9 January 1969, p. 51.

Lay, M. (1968), 'Kindergarten "learning to learn" program evaluation', in *Final Report, Project Headstart Research and Evaluation Center, Syracuse University*.

Levin, H. (1966), 'Child-rearing antecedents of cognitive behaviour', in *Learning about Learning. Report of the Working Conference on Research on Children's Learning*, U.S. Govt. Printing Office.

Levine, S. (1960), 'Stimulation in infancy', *Scient. Amer.*, May. Reprinted in *Psychobiology*, Freeman & Co., 1966.

Lilley, I. M. (1967), *Friedrich Froebel*, Cambridge University Press.

Lipsitt, L. P. (1963), 'Learning in the first year of life', in L. P. Lipsitt and C. C. Spiker (eds.), *Advances in Child Development and Behaviour*, vol. 1, Academic Press.

Lipsitt, L. P. (1967), 'The concepts of development and learning in child behaviour', in D. B. Lindsley and A. A. Lumsdaine (eds.), *Brain Function and Learning. UCLA Forum in Medical Sciences*, vol. 4, University of California Press.

Maccoby, E. E., Dowley, E. M., Hagen, J. W., and **Degerman, R.** (1965), 'Activity level and intellectual functioning in normal pre-school children', *Child Dev.*, vol. 36, pp. 761–70.

Maizels, J. (1961), *Two to Five in High Flats*, The Housing Centre, London.

Mason, S. (1960), *Health and Hormones*, Penguin Books.

McConville, M. (1968), 'High society', *Observer*, 18 February 1968.

McCullough, M. (1969), 'Therapeutic playgroup', *New Society*, 9 January 1969, pp. 50–51.

McGaugh, J., Weinberger, N., and **Whalen, R.** (eds.) (1966), *Psychobiology. The Biological Base of Behaviour*, W. H. Freeman & Co.

McMillan, M. (1927a), *The Life of Rachel McMillan*, Dent.

McMillan, M. (1927b), *The Nursery School*, Dent.

Meyer, W. J., and **Egeland, B.** (1968), 'Changes in Stanford Binet I.Q. performance vs. competence', in *Final Report, Project Headstart Research and Evaluation Center, Syracuse University.*

Montessori, M. (1912), *The Montessori Method*, Frederick A. Stockes. (Reprinted by Schocken Books, N.Y., 1964.)

Dr Montessori's Own Handbook, Schocken Books, 1965.

Moore, S. B., and **Richards, P.** (1959), *Teaching in the Nursery School*, Harper, N.Y., 1959.

Moss, H. A., and **Kagan, J.** (1958), 'Maternal influences on early I.Q. scores', *Psychol. Rep.*, vol. 4, pp. 655–61.

Newman, H. H., Freeman, F. N., and **Holzinger, K. J.** (1937), *Twins: a Study of Heredity and Environment*, University of Chicago Press.

Newson, J. and E. (1968), *Four-year-old in an Urban Community*, Allen and Unwin.

Norcross, K. J., and **Spiker, C. C.** (1957), 'The effects of type of stimulus pretraining on discrimination performance in pre-school children', *Child Dev.*, vol. 28, pp. 79–84.

Not Yet Five, Ministries of Education and Health, H.M.S.O., 1942.

Olson, J., and **Larson, R.** (1962), *A Pilot Study Evaluating One Method of Teaching Culturally Deprived Children*, Racine, Wisconsin (mimeographed).

Olson, W. C. (1957), Psychological foundations of the curriculum, UNESCO, *Educational Studies and Documents*, no. 26, Paris.

Organisation of Pre-primary Education, UNESCO publication no. 230, Geneva.

O'Sullivan, D. (1957–8), A comparative study of two groups of children in the infant school: (1) Nursery children (2) Non-nursery children. *Unpublished Thesis. Child Development Centre, Institute of Education, University of London.*

Owen, R. (1927), *A New View of Society and Other Writings*, Dent.

Packman, J. (1968), *Child Care: Needs and Numbers*, Allen & Unwin.

Papousek, H. (1965), 'The development of higher nervous activity in children in the first half-year of life', *Monogr. Soc. Res. Child Dev.*, vol. 30, no. 2.

Peterson, T. J. (1937), 'A preliminary study of the effects of previous nursery school attendance upon five-year-old children entering kindergarten', *Univ. of Iowa Stud. in child Welf.*, vol. 14, pp. 197–248.

Pines, M. (1969), *Revolution in Learning. The Years from Birth to Five*, Allen Lane The Penguin Press.

Pre-school Education. Statistical Reports and Studies, UNESCO, 1963.

Primary Education in Wales (The Gittins Report), Central Advisory Council for Education (Wales), H.M.S.O., 1967.

Pringle, M. L. K., and **Tanner, M.** (1965), 'The effects of early deprivation on speech development', in *Deprivation and Education*, Longmans.

Project in Compensatory Education, Field Report no. 6. Schools Council, 1968.

Rapier, J. L. (1962), 'Measured intelligence and the ability to learn', *Acta Psychol.*, vol. 20, pp. 1–17.

Read, K. H. (1960), *The Nursery School: A Human Relations Laboratory*, Saunders.

Report of the Consultative Committee on the Primary School (Hadow Report), H.M.S.O., 1931.

Report of the Enquiry into the Collapse of Flats at Ronan Point, Canning Town, Ministry of Housing and Local Government, H.M.S.O., 1968.

Rheingold, H. L. (1960), 'The measurement of maternal care', *Child Dev.*, vol. 31, pp. 565–75.

Rhinehart, J. B. (1942), 'Some effects of a nursery school education program on a group of three-year-olds', *J. genet. Psychol.*, vol. 65, pp. 153–61.

Robertson, A. (1966), 'Cortical neurones', *Science Journal*, Associated Illiffe Press.

Rose, S. (1966), *The Chemistry of Life*, Penguin Books.

Rosenblith, J. F. (1959), 'Learning by imitation in kindergarten children', *Child Dev.*, vol. 30, pp. 69–80.

Rudolph, M. (1954), *Living and Learning in Nursery School*, Harper.

Saguisag, B. V. (1960), 'The effect of kindergarten and non-kindergarten education on the achievement of pupils in the primary department of the Phillipines Women's University', *Education Abstracts: Pre-school Education*, vol. 12, no. 1.

Schaeffer, M. S., and **Gerjuoy, I. R.** (1955), 'The effect of stimulus naming on the discrimination learning of kindergarten children', *Child Dev.*, vol. 26, pp. 231–40.

Schwarz, J. C. (1968), 'Presence of an attached peer and security in a novel environment', in *Final Report, Project Headstart Research and Evaluation Center, Syracuse University*.

Scott, J. P. (1962), 'Critical periods in behavioural development', *Science*, vol. 138, pp. 949–58.

Sears, P. S., and **Dowley, E. M.** (1963), 'Research on teaching in the nursery school', in N. L. Gage (ed.), *Handbook of Research on Teaching*, Rand McNally.

Seebohm Committee Report on Local Authority and Allied Personal Social Services, Commd 3703, H.M.S.O., 1968.

Shearer, A. (1969), 'Closed for lack of a lavatory', *Guardian*, 17 January 1969.

Shirley, M. M. (1931–3), *The First Two Years: A Study of Twenty-five Babies*, 2 vols., University of Minnesota Press.

Siegel, A. E., and **Haas, M. B.** (1963), 'The working mother: a review of research', *Child Dev.*, vol. 34, pp. 513–42.

Sluckin, W. (1965), *Imprinting and Early Learning*, Methuen.

Standing, E. M. (1957), *Maria Montessori: Her Life and Work*, Hollis & Carter.

Starkweather, E. K., and **Roberts, K.** (1940), 'I.Q. changes occurring during nursery school attendance at the Merrill–Palmer Institute School', *39th Yearbook Nat. Soc. Studies Educ.*, part 2, pp. 315–35.

The State of Nursery Education, National Union of Teachers, 1964.

Stern, C., and **Keislar, E. R.** (1967), 'Acquisition of problem-solving strategies by young children and its relation to mental age', *Amer. educ. Res. J.*, vol. 4, pp. 1–12.

Szentágothai, Flerkó, Mess, and **Halász** (1968), *Hypothalamic Control of the Anterior Pituitary*, Akadémiai Kiadó, Budapest.

Tanner, J. M. (1961), *Education and Physical Growth*, University of London Press.

Tanner, J. M. (1968), 'Earlier malnutrition in man', *Scient. Amer.*, vol. 218, no. 1, W. H. Freeman & Co.

Thompson, W. R. (1965), 'The behaviour of offspring', *Science Journal*, Associated Illiffe Press.

Thomson, W. R., and **Heron, W.** (1954), 'The effects of restricting experience in dogs', *Canad. J. Psychol.*, vol. 8, pp. 17–31.

Todd, V. E., and **Heffernan, H.** (1964), *The Years Before School: Guiding Pre-school Children*, Macmillan.

Townsend, P. (1967), *Poverty, Socialism and Labour in Power*, Fabian Tract no. 371.

Trasler, G. *et al.* (1968), *The Formative Years*, B.B.C.

Trends in Education, Department of Education and Science, H.M.S.O., 1966.

Universal Opportunities of Early Childhood Education, Education Policies Commission, National Education Association, Washington, 1966.

The Use of Rhesus Monkeys in the Study of Mother–Infant Interaction, Current Medical Research, H.M.S.O., 1968.

Van Alstyne, D., and **Hattwick, L. A.** (1939), 'A follow-up study of the behaviour of nursery school children', *Child Dev.*, vol. 10, pp. 43–72.

Van der Eyken, W. (1968), in F. J. Adams *et al.* (eds.), *The Geography of Deprivation*.

Van der Eyken, W., and **Turner, B.** (1969), *Adventures in Education*, Allen Lane The Penguin Press.

Vernon, J. (1966), 'Sensory deprivation', *Science Journal*, Illiffe Press.

Vitz, P. C. (1960–61), 'Some changes in the behaviour of nursery school children over a period of seven weeks', *J. nursery Educ.*, vol. 16, pp. 62–5.

Vygotski, L. S. (1962), *Thought and Language*, M.I.T. Press.

Walsh, M. E. (1931), 'The relation of nursery-school training to development of certain personality traits', *Child Dev.*, vol. 2, pp. 72–9.

Wann, K. D., Dorn, M. S., and **Liddle, E. A.** (1962), *Fostering Intellectual Development in Young Children*, Teachers College, Columbia University.

Wellman, B. L. (1932), 'The effect of pre-school attendance upon I.Q.', *J. exper. Educ.*, vol. 2, pp. 48–69.

Wellman, B. L. (1943), 'The effects of pre-school attendance upon intellectual development', in R. G. Barker, J. S. Kounin and H. F. Wright (eds.), *Child Behaviour and Development*, McGraw-Hill.

Wellman, B. L. (1945), 'I.Q. changes of pre-school and non-pre-school groups during the pre-school years: A summary of the literature', *J. Psychol.*, vol. 20, pp. 347–68.

Wellman, B. L., and **Pegram, E. L.** (1945), 'Binet I.Q. changes of orphanage pre-school children: A re-analysis', *J. genet. Psychol.*, vol. 65, pp. 239–63.

White, B. L., Castle, P., and **Held, R.** (1964), 'Observations on the development of visually directed teaching', *Child Dev.*, vol. 35, pp. 349–64.

White, B. L., and **Held, R.** (1966), 'Plasticity of sensorimotor development in the human infant', in J. F. Rosenblith and W. Allinsmith (eds.), *The Causes of Behaviour: Readings in Child Development and Educational Psychology*, Allyn & Bacon.

Whiteman, M., Brown, B., and **Deutsch, M.** (1966), 'Some effects of social class and race on children's language and intellectual abilities', in *Studies in Deprivation*, Institute for Developmental Studies, N.Y.

Willis, M. (1953), *Play Areas on Housing Estates*, H.M.S.O.

Witte, Pastor (1913), *The Education of Karl Witte, or the Training of a Child* (trans. L. Weiner), Harrap.

Wolfhein, N. (1953), *Psychology in the Nursery School*, Duckworth.

Women and Children in the U.S.S.R.: Brief Statistical Returns, Foreign Languages Publishing House, Moscow, 1963.

Yudkin, S. (1967), *0 - 5. A Report on the Care of Pre-school Children. National Society of Children's Nurseries*, Allen & Unwin.

Zimiles, H. (1968), Problems of assessment of academic and intellectual variables, *Paper Presented to a Symposium on 'Problems of Educational Evaluation Confronted in Headstart'*, Chicago, February 1968.

Zimiles, H. (1968), 'An analysis of current issues in the evaluation of educational programs', in J. Hellmuth (ed.), *The Disadvantaged Child*, Special Child Publications, Seattle.

Organizations

The following organizations carry out activities involving the provision for the pre-school child and its mother in Great Britain.

Advisory Centre for Education, 57 Russell Street, Cambridge.

Association of Child Care Officers, Bernhard Baron Settlement, Berner Street, London E.1.

Association of Children's Officers, Hon. Secretary, E. P. Brown, Children's Department, Polebarn House, Polebarn Road, Trowbridge, Wilts.

Association of Psychiatric Social Workers, Oxford House, Mape Street, London E.2.

Association of Social Workers, 296 Vauxhall Bridge Road, London S.W.1.

Children's Aid Society, 55 Leigham Court Road, London S.W.16.

Children's Country Holidays Fund, 1 York Street, London W.1.

Church of England Children's Society, Old Town Hall, Kennington Road, London S.E.11.

Church of England Board for Social Responsibility, Church House, Dean's Yard, London S.W.1.

Church of Scotland Committee on Social Service, 121 George Street, Edinburgh 2.

Council for Children's Welfare, 23 Marlborough Place, London N.W.8.

Crusade of Rescue and Homes for Destitute Catholic Children, 73 St Charles Square, London W.10.

Dr Barnardo's, 18 Stepney Causeway, London E.1.

Fairbridge Society, Northeast Wing, Bush House, Aldwych, London W.C.2.

Family Service Units, 207 Marylebone Road, London N.W.1.

Federation of Committees for the Moral Welfare of Children, 8 Palace Gate, London W.8.

Friends of the Children Society, Annexe Factory, Wood Lane Sidings, London W.12.

Health Visitors Association, 36 Eccleston Square, London S.W.1.

Housing Centre Trust, 13 Suffolk Street, London S.W.1.

International Help for Children, 42 Maiden Lane, London W.C.2.

Invalid Children's Aid Association, 4 Palace Gate, London W.8.

Jewish Welfare Board, 74a Charlotte Street, London W.1.

Kindergartens for Commerce, 59 Rectory Road, Beckenham, Kent.

Mothers' Union, Mary Sumner House, Tufton Street, London S.W.1.

National Adoption Society, 47a Manchester Street, London W.1.

National Association for Maternal and Child Welfare, B.M.A. House, Tavistock Square, London W.C.1.

National Association for Mental Health, 39 Queen Anne Street, London W.1.

National Association of Pre-School Playgroups, Toynbee Hall, 28 Commercial Street, London E.1.

National Bureau for Co-operation in Child Care, Adam House, 1 Fitzroy Square, London W.1.

National Children's Adoption Association, 71 Knightsbridge, London S.W.1.

National Children's Home and Orphanage, 85 Highbury Park, London N.5.

National Committee for Commonwealth Immigrants, 33 Sackville Street, London W.1.

National Council for the Unmarried Mother and Her Child, 255 Kentish Town Road, London N.W.5.

National Council of Social Service, 26 Bedford Square, London W.C.1.

National Council of Voluntary Child Care Associations, Hon. Chairman, Canon Phillip Harvey, Crusade of Rescue, 73 St Charles Square, London W.10.

National Council of Women of Great Britain, 36 Lower Sloane Square, London S.W.1.

National Deaf Children's Society, 31 Gloucester Place, London W.1.

National Society for Autistic Children, 100 Wise Lane, London N.W.7.

National Society of Children's Nurseries, 45 Russell Street, London W.C.1.

National Campaign for Nursery Education, Mrs V. Ross, Flat 9, 26 Highbury Grove, London N.5.

National Society for Mentally Handicapped Children, 5 Bulstrode Street, London W.1.

National Society for the Prevention of Cruelty to Children, 1 Riding House Street, London W.1.

Nursery School Association of Great Britain and Northern Ireland, 89 Stamford Street, London S.E.1.

Quarrier's Homes, Bridge of Weir, Renfrewshire.

Register for Qualified Married Women, 1 Dunsany Road, London W.14.

Royal Scottish Society for Prevention of Cruelty to Children, 16 Melville Street, Edinburgh 3.

Salvation Army International Headquarters, 101 Queen Victoria Street, London E.C.4.

Save the Children Fund, 29 Queen Anne's Gate, London S.W.1.

Scottish Association for the Adoption of Children, 2 Coates Crescent, Edinburgh 3.

Scottish Council for the Care of Spastics, 22 Corstorphine Road, Edinburgh 12.

Scottish Council for the Unmarried Mother and Her Child, 30 Castle Street, Edinburgh 2.

Scottish Society for Mentally Handicapped Children,
69 West Regent Street, Glasgow C.2.

Society of Medical Officers of Health, Tavistock House South,
Tavistock Square, London W.C.1.

Special Schools Association, c/o 46 Balliol Avenue, London E.4.

Standing Conference of Societies Registered for Adoption,
Gort Lodge, Petersham, Surrey.

The Spastics Society, 12 Park Crescent, London W.1.

Further Reading

A. Denny, *Children in Need,* S.C.M. Press, n.d.
A revealing study of the social and psychological deprivation of the young in our society.

D. E. M. Gardner, *The Children's Play Centre,* Methuen, 1935.
An analysis of children's problems as seen through their play activities. A simple guide to the nature of much of the activity in any good nursery school or class.

D. E. M. Gardner, *The Education of Young Children,* Methuen, 1956.
A simply written but expert study that includes chapters on parents, their children's problems and the principles of preparing for work in nursery schools.

R. D. Hess and **R. Meyer Bear** (eds.), *Early Education: A Comprehensive Evaluation of Current Theory, Research and Practice,* Aldine Publishing Co., 1968.
For those who want to immerse themselves in the subject, here is the best current survey of the field, with a copious bibliography and contributions from a score of the leading U.S. practitioners. Not easy going, but authoritative.

E. Howe, *Under Five,* Conservative Political Centre, London, 1966.
A layman's guide through the morass of legislation and public and private provision for nursery schooling and its ancillaries. Its statistics are only superseded by the more recently published figures in the Plowden Report (see References).

S. Isaacs, *The Nursery Years: The Mind of the Child from Birth to Six Years,* Routledge & Kegan Paul, 1929.
An incomparable parental guide, as true today as when it was written during the final years of the Malting House School experiment.

E. Lawrence (ed.), *Friedrich Froebel and the English Education,* University of London Press, 1952.
A fascinating and popular collection of essays that gives a glimpse of the aims of at least one pioneer in the education of the young.

E. M. Matterson, *Play with a Purpose for Under-Sevens,*
Penguin Books, 1965.
Faced with an absence of playgroups and nursery school facilities,
frustrated parents will turn to this splendid guide for a hatful of
ideas on how to provide a stimulating environment for their own
youngsters. Afterwards they may well wonder what on earth they
ever did with their spare time, now totally devoted to knocking up
Wendy houses and designing Red Indian regalia.

D. May, *Children in the Nursery School: Studies in Personal
Adjustment in Early Childhood,* University of London Press, 1963.
A study by a pupil of Susan Isaacs at the Child Development
Centre, London University, illuminating some of the social
problems that face young children.

National Union of Teachers, *The State of Nursery Education,*
1964.
A report of a survey carried out by the N.U.T. in 1962 into the
facilities available and the demand for the education of the
pre-school child.

M. Pines, *Revolution in Learning: The Years from Birth to Five,*
Allen Lane The Penguin Press, 1969.
An American look, first published in 1967, at the changing ideas on
pre-school learning in the U.S. Very readable, with first-hand
accounts of some of the experiments now under way.

S. Yudkin, *0 – 5: A Report on the Care of Pre-School Children,*
Allen & Unwin Ltd on behalf of the National Society of Children's
Nurseries.
A cogent enquiry, containing a great deal of basic information,
carried out by a Working Party under the chairmanship of the late
Dr Simon Yudkin. Brief (seventy pages) but readable and still very
relevant.